THE PRAYER OF SILENCE

D1643090

ALEXANDER RYRIE

SLG Press

Convent of the Incarnation Fairacres
Parker Street Oxford OX4 1TB England

www.slgpress.co.uk

First published by SLG Press, 2012

© ALEXANDER RYRIE, 2012

Cover illustration:
© Angelika Thiermann, 2012:
Omapere, Hokianga, New Zealand

ISBN: 978-0-7283-0239-6

ISSN: 0307-1405

All rights reserved

SLG Press asserts:

(a)   on behalf of Alexander Ryrie, the moral right of Alexander Ryrie to be identified as the author of the work, in accordance with Sections 77 & 78 of the Copyright, Designs and Patents Act 1988;

(b)   on behalf of Angelika Thiermann, the moral right of Angelika Thiermann to be identified as the author of the photographic work on the cover, in accordance with Sections 77 & 78 of the Copyright, Designs and Patents Act 1988.

Printed by Joshua Horgan   Oxford   England

FOREWORD

WITHIN the hub of international diplomacy that is the United Nations Headquarters in New York there is a small, still, silent dark room with one shaft of light striking a raised rock in the centre. It has become a place for people of many faiths, and none, to encounter silence.

Our being brought to the place of silence comes in various ways. Caught up in the social activism of the 1960s and early 1970s, I became physically and emotionally exhausted and disheartened. I made my way to the Cistercian monastery of Mount St Bernard Abbey, where I experienced an unexpected inner homecoming. I encountered silence and a sense of mystery, the all-pervading presence of God in creation and within the deep places of our humanity.

Do we have to go to a monastery to encounter silence? Do we have to go away in order to come to our place of inner necessity, our inner cave? The prayer of silence *where we are* awakens a deeper attentiveness, a listening for the pulse, the heartbeat, of God within the heart of the world.

Some of us are drawn into an unanticipated and unwelcome solitude, experienced through physical frailty, illness, bereavement, divorce, imprisonment. To embrace silence within these raw and scary terrains is to be brought to the core of our being. It is to stand utterly unprotected before God.

I live with a serious degenerative spinal condition, and pain belongs to my experience of the night. As a result of correspondence with others for whom the night also holds a turbulent, noisy silence, I approached the Sisters of the Love of God at Fairacres in Oxford, since they have a tradition of prayer in the night. They in turn suggested that I write to

Sandy Ryrie. He introduced me to his writings, *Prayer in the Night*[1] and *Silent Waiting*.[2]

Sandy's series of papers on 'The Prayer of Silence' have been a godsend to many. The papers are short, yet long enough; they go deep, yet remain succinct. They provide clarity, while embracing mystery. He writes of the indescribable and unknowable depths. His invitation is to enter the silence and to be met by the One who is 'infinitely beyond us yet intimately close within us' (p. 31). He helps us to understand the roots and meaning of Hebrew words. Some of his sentences are breathtaking. His wisdom is learned through the encounter with the silent God.

Those of us who have been nourished by Sandy's occasional papers welcome the publication of these gems, trusting that others will experience a renewal of heart—and enter the paradox of being offered a vocabulary for our wordless prayer of silence.

Donald Eadie
Chairman of the Birmingham District
of the Methodist Church 1987-96
November 2012

---

[1] *Prayer of the Heart: An Approach to Silent Prayer & Prayer in the Night*, Alexander Ryrie, SLG Press, 2002, and also in e-book formats.
[2] *Silent Waiting: The Biblical Roots of Contemplative Spirituality*, Alexander Ryrie, Canterbury Press, 1999.

CONTENTS

III. RESPONDING TO GOD

IV. WITH OTHERS ON THE HEART

INTRODUCTION

THIS BOOK is a collection of occasional short papers on how silent prayer can assist and enable the inner or spiritual life. The papers were originally written separately, and they were distributed to a number of interested people over a ten-year period. They have now been grouped and arranged around four themes. Because of the way in which they originated, there is some repetition of thoughts and ideas. I therefore suggest that readers may find it helpful to use this book as a form of spiritual reading, selecting a particular chapter at a time.

I am grateful to Sister Avis Mary and her colleagues at SLG Press for taking the time and trouble to prepare these papers for publication. I want also to thank the original recipients of the papers, whose warm appreciation encouraged me to continue writing them. I hope that other readers might now find them helpful in same way.

Sandy Ryrie
November 2012

THE PRAYER OF SILENCE

I

FOR GOD ALONE

1.

The Magnetism of God

SISTER JANE of the Sisters of the Love of God once wrote of this 'utterly magnetic God'.[1] There is a magnetism in God—a wonderful, mysterious something, which draws and attracts and pulls us. Like all magnetic forces, it is hidden and unseen; and so it can go unrecognised, and be ignored, forgotten or doubted. We are not always aware of it, and some people never are; but it is there, constant, unceasing and inexorable. So, at least from time to time, if not all of the time, we can find ourselves conscious of this magnetic something, the pull of the unyielding love of God, tugging at the centre of our hearts, drawing us towards God.

This magnetism has the effect of turning us towards God. The Bible speaks frequently of turning, using a Hebrew word which means to turn, return or repent. It is used both of God and of human beings. God turns to us in humility, patience and love, and we are invited to turn, or return, to God and to repent. Our relationship with God, our being in God, grows and develops as God turns to us in love and we turn to God. As the needle of the compass is turned towards the pole, or as a flower turns towards the sun, so by God's magnetism we are turned and drawn to God.

To turn in this way is to pray. When we pray, we turn, or rather we are turned, towards God. It is only because of God's magnetism that we are moved to pray at all, for it is God who turns and draws us. To pray is to yield to this magnetic power, to allow ourselves to be turned and drawn towards God. By setting aside a time of silent prayer, we are seeking to provide an opportunity for God's magnetism to work on us and draw our hearts closer to God. Often we are not aware of it, and don't know what God is doing, for God's

---

[1] Sister Jane SLG, *Loving God Whatever*, SLG Press, 2nd ed. 2008, p. 59.

magnetic power remains mysterious and hidden, and operates without our knowledge; but by holding ourselves still in expectation we are opening ourselves to it.

We can, of course, turn to God in various ways and at any time, not only in times of deliberate silent prayer. At other times, in the midst of the busyness and activity of the day, or in the mysteriously rich but sometimes frightening silence of the night, we can let ourselves feel the magnetism of God, however briefly, and be turned towards it. If we are open to it, the sudden pull of God can catch us unawares in the midst of everyday life.

Magnetism has also a contrary aspect. A magnet not only attracts but repels; it both draws and pushes away. When we are drawn to God, some other things get pushed aside. Turning to God involves turning away, not from all worldly things, but from those things which draw us away from God—things which falsely claim to give us security, or which seek to dominate our lives or give them a spurious purpose. To turn in this way is to repent—not in the sense of remorse and beating the breast, but in the biblical sense of turning away from things that would ensnare us, and turning towards God. When by God's magnetism we are drawn closer to God, these things begin to lose some of their opposing magnetic power.

All this happens because there are aspects of ourselves that respond to God's magnetism. Maybe it is a sense of inner emptiness—what R. S. Thomas calls 'the emptiness without him of my whole being'.[2] Maybe it is an awareness, however dim, that God is all that we need, our beginning and our end, our source and our goal, our being and our life, our peace and our security, our treasure and our joy. In the silence of prayer we seek to open these hidden aspects of ourselves to 'this utterly magnetic God'.

---

[2] 'The Absence', *Collected Poems 1945-90*, R. S. Thomas.

2.

For God Alone

ONE OF the distinctive things about silent prayer is that it is focussed on God alone. There are, of course, other kinds of prayer, such as prayer in which we bring our thoughts and concerns to God. It is right and proper that we should give thanks for good things, and that we should present to God our own needs and deepest wishes, and our concerns and petitions for other people. Sometimes it is only after we have offered our prayers of this kind that we can move into a mode of prayer which concentrates, not on our concerns and needs, but simply on God alone. For the prayer of silence moves beyond these other prayers. It is done, not for our sake, but for God's. In it we try to remember God, to think only of God, to give God our whole attention, to place ourselves in God's presence, to hold ourselves still before God and to offer our whole being to God.

This is what contemplation means: focussing on God alone. Evelyn Underhill writes:

> By contemplative prayer I mean the sort of prayer which aims at God in and for himself, and not for any of his gifts whatever, and more and more profoundly rests in him alone.[3]

According to the author of *The Cloud of Unknowing*, the prayer of contemplation requires 'a naked intention towards God and himself alone'.[4] Elsewhere he says:

---

[3] *Concerning the Inner Life,* Evelyn Underhill, Methuen, 1924, p. 8.
[4] *The Cloud of Unknowing,* Penguin Classics, pp. 61, 69.

Mean God, and not what you get out of him. Indeed, hate to think of anything but God himself, so that nothing occupies your mind or will but only God.

To concentrate solely on God is not something that comes easily to most of us. But we should note that the author of *The Cloud* speaks of our 'intention'. The important thing is that our *intention* should be to focus on God alone, that we should *'mean* God'. And the pursuit of this intention will gradually make the concentration easier. We should also note that our intention should be *'towards* God', in God's direction. We can't see God, but we can learn increasingly to direct our attention towards God. 'Contemplation', says K. E. Kirk, 'is not so much "looking *at* God" as "looking *towards* God"'.[5]

Some people find that it helps them to look towards God if they focus their closed eyes and keep them still. Many are also helped by a 'rhythm prayer', a few brief words repeated over and over again, usually in rhythm with one's breathing. The value of such a prayer is not only that it helps us to quieten ourselves, but also that it helps us to focus on God. That's why it is important that the words we repeat should be a *prayer*, words addressed to God, so that they draw our attention towards God, and God alone.

Prayer in this mode may seem difficult, but in one sense it is easy, or at least simple, for it means simply being still in God's presence and letting God take over. And it is liberating. In this prayer we move beyond the cares of every day (which we will already have offered to God) and, as Evelyn Underhill said, 'more and more profoundly rest in him alone'.

---

[5] *The Vision of God*, K. E. Kirk, Longmans, 1931, p. 94.

3.

Desire for God

SILENT PRAYER is an expression of a desire for God. The first commandment is that we should love God, and a large part of love is desire. We are told to love God with all our heart and soul and mind and strength—with everything we've got. Love is not a cold, rational, dispassionate thing, inspired by duty. Love of God does indeed involve our mind and our strength, but it springs essentially from the feeling heart. It is warm and passionate, inspired by a longing and desire for the living God.

Nowhere do we find this desire and longing given better expression than in the Psalms. 'My soul thirsts for you, my flesh faints for you, as in a dry and weary land where there is no water.'[6] Desire arises in our 'soul', our inner secret being, and affects our 'flesh', all our outer life. Desire is like thirst—a powerful image in a hot, dry land: 'My soul longs for you, O God. My soul thirsts for God, for the living God.'[7] God, says the Psalmist, is our 'portion'[8]—the one thing given us as a resource out of which we are to build our life; so God is our one basic need, the 'one thing' we ask and seek after. The desire for God supersedes all other things, and before it all other desires grow dim: 'Having you, there is nothing on earth that I desire.'[9] You are my God, says the Psalmist repeatedly. You, the Almighty, Eternal Creator, are my God, the source and object of my longing and desire.

Every living person has a desire for God, although they may not recognise it as such. Deep within each of us there is a

---

[6] Ps. 63: 1.
[7] Ps. 42: 1-2.
[8] Ps. 16: 5; 119: 57; 142: 5.
[9] Ps. 73: 25 (my translation).

longing for something beyond ourselves which gives purpose and meaning and fulfilment to life, a longing prompted by the God who is the source and the end of our life. With many people it seems to find expression in a desire for other things, or perhaps simply in an inner restlessness and a longing for they know not what. And even those who recognise and acknowledge their desire are not aware of it all the time. The desire for God may be hidden away within us, so that we are not conscious of it. As an old Scottish crofter's peat fire was 'smoored' with ashes overnight, but was stirred into flame again in the morning, so our desire for God is often 'smoored' and covered over by the ordinary things of life which are at the forefront of our attention.

The purpose of silent prayer is to let ourselves be drawn to the God who is the desire of our hearts. Of course, even in our times of prayer we may not be conscious of a desire for God. But in prayer we give attention to God, not so much through the workings of our minds, as with our hearts, the place of our longing. In this way we make room for the desire for God. By allowing our thoughts to centre on God, our eyes to focus on God and our ears to listen to the silence of God, we allow the desire to grow within us. In the prayer of silence we are quietly nurturing our deep, hidden desire for God, keeping it at least smouldering, even when it is not burning brightly.

And there can come times when the flame bursts out, when our desire quickens and we feel an ardent longing for God. Then we become aware again that God is indeed the desire of our hearts, our inheritance and our portion, our treasure and our delight, our beginning and our end, and we know that deep within us, even when we are scarcely aware of it, our inner being longs and thirsts for the living God. It is a longing and desire that never finds complete fulfilment in this life; we go on longing and yearning for God. But this very desire, nurtured by silent prayer, gives life its meaning, its purpose and some of its deepest joy.

4.

I and You

THERE IS all the difference between talking about someone when he or she is not there and being with that person face to face. Even if we are not saying anything, the presence of the person changes the way we are towards him or her. It alters our stance in relation to the person. Being 'before the face' of someone, having that person's face in front of us, changes him or her from being 'he' or 'she' to being 'you'.

Properly and strictly speaking we should not talk of God in the third person. God is always present, and so is always 'You'. We are never in a situation when God is absent, so that we can talk of God as 'he' or 'she', as if God were not there. When we do so, we make God into an object, something apart from ourselves that we can think about, talk about, remember or forget, summon or dismiss, attend to or ignore. This happens all the time, in our talk about God, our theological books, even to some extent in our worship: God becomes a 'he' out there. This is to some extent unavoidable. Because of the nature of our human minds and of our language, we cannot help talking of God in this way. But it is important every now and then to remind ourselves that God is not 'he' or 'she' (let alone 'it'!), but 'Thou', or 'You', a 'Person' who is always present with us.

We have a good example in St Augustine's *Confessions*, a long book containing a lot of theology as well as his own personal story, all of it addressed to God in the second person. God is called 'You' throughout; a reminder that we live our lives and think our thoughts always (in the language of the Bible) 'before God's face'. There is no escaping the face of God. In the words of Psalm 139, 'Whither shall I flee from thy presence?'—literally, 'thy face'.

Prayer is a matter of changing from talking about God as 'he' or 'she' to being aware of God as 'Thou' or 'You'. All spoken prayer is addressed *to* God in the second person. But silent prayer is also, and in a special way, *about* God in the second person. The prayer of silence is a matter of quietly remembering that God is in the room, and adjusting our thoughts, our attitudes, our behaviour, our inner and outer being, to take account of this.

We can do this at any time. The 'You-ness' of God can accompany us in the midst of life, or can be recalled at particular moments. But there is value in placing ourselves more deliberately and exclusively before this 'You-ness' for a chosen spell. By shutting out everything else and focussing entirely on God as 'You' for a little while, we can deepen the mysterious inner sense of a relationship which can only be described as an 'I-Thou' or 'I-You' relationship.

Strangely, this sense of God as 'You' has the effect of giving us a deeper sense of ourselves as 'I' or 'Me'. Being with this 'You', I know myself really to be 'Me'. It is the presence of the 'You' that establishes and confirms the 'Me'. Who I am, and what I am here for, remains in part a mystery. But the mystery is illumined, and I become truly 'Me' when I am set in this presence. The French philosopher Paul Ricoeur has said that, when we address ourselves to God, 'There is henceforth an "I" because there is a "Thou".'[10] The mysterious sense of being with a 'You' makes me into 'Me', and makes it all right and acceptable for me to be 'Me'. The anxieties and perplexities of who we are and what our life is about get swallowed up by the living reality of the 'You' who remains separate from us, but is deeply close to us. Before 'You', I become 'I'. This is part of the deep reality of silent prayer.

---

[10] *The Symbolism of Evil*, Paul Ricoeur.

12

5.

Companionship

SILENT PRAYER leads towards a companionship with God of a unique and special nature, a friendship both of mysterious intimacy and of wonder and awe. The Bible describes this in a number of ways. Figures of olden time, Enoch and Noah, were said to have 'walked with God'.[11] Abraham, the father of three faiths, was known throughout the generations as 'the friend of God'.[12] The Psalmist declared that those who revere God are taken into friendship with God and taught God's covenant.[13] Jesus called his disciples 'friends', not servants.[14] Ever since then, people of prayer have found that in a strange way God becomes their companion and friend.

As we make a practice of holding ourselves still and open before God, we are drawn into a relationship with God as our companion. Of course, we are not always conscious of this companionship. In much of life, our minds are occupied with other things, and our attention is not on the God who walks beside us. We forget, and may sometimes doubt, God's presence. But as we persevere in prayer, as we remain constant in our determination to wait upon God, we can find that our sense of God's constant companionship grows. If we develop the use of a rhythm prayer, not only at specific times which we set aside for prayer, but also in odd moments throughout the day and night, we may be granted a greater awareness of the companionship of the God who accompanies us in all the circumstances of life.

---

[11] Gen. 5: 22, 24; 6: 9.
[12] 2 Chron. 20: 7; Isa. 41: 8; Jas. 2: 23, and *Koran* 4: 125.
[13] Ps. 25: 14.
[14] John 15: 15.

It is a companionship of mysterious intimacy. It is a walk with One who is closer to us than we are to ourselves, who knows our thoughts before they reach the surface of our minds, who understands the feelings of our hearts, who hears our words uttered in secrecy and reads our wordless silences. Our secrets are bared, our hidden weaknesses uncovered, and the things of which we are ashamed are both exposed and accepted. God walks beside us, whether we remember the presence of God or not. We are often unaware of this companionship, but from time to time we may sense the warmth and the assurance of an inner presence.

It is also a companionship of wonder and awe. We walk with the unknown God. Our companion is none other than the Infinite, Eternal, Transcendent God, our Maker and the Creator of heaven and earth, totally other in nature, infinitely beyond us in being and in magnificence and holiness, whose dwelling is beyond the galaxies, outside the created world of space and time. We cannot imagine the mystery of God's being, and so we may sometimes forget the wonder and awe of this companionship and the holiness of the One with whom we walk. Our journey with God may often seem ordinary, routine and unexciting. But there may be times of wonder and awe, when the majesty of God breaks in upon us, occasions when with reverence we touch transcendence and glimpse the hidden splendour of another world.

This companionship is God's gift, and it is God who deepens and strengthens it. As we persist in prayer, God draws us more deeply into this friendship, so that it becomes both more intimate and more filled with wonder and awe. We embrace God more warmly in our inner heart; we bow more deeply in reverence at the mystery of the transcendence; and we are drawn ever closer towards our 'utterly magnetic God'.[15]

---

[15] Sister Jane SLG, *Loving God Whatever*, SLG Press, 2nd ed. 2008, p. 59.

6.

A Reciprocal Relationship

ONE OF the deeper aspects of the prayer of silence is that, by it, we may find ourselves drawn into a relationship with God which is one of intimacy and reciprocity.

This relationship happens in our hearts, our inmost selves, where we are truly ourselves. Here, in our hidden selves, in the place which no one else can enter and the depths of which we ourselves do not fully know, God engages in a silent, unspoken dialogue with us. Most of the time we are not aware of this dialogue; it goes on in secret. Silent prayer is a way of listening in to this dialogue; of making ourselves aware that God is relating to us at the deepest level; and of entering this relationship.

God is the Lord God Almighty, infinite in greatness, ineffable and holy, whom we cannot grasp or comprehend with our minds, yet God is present in the secret depths of the individual human being. The God who is 'greater than suns or stars' is also 'closer than breathing'. God is closer to us than we are to ourselves, engaging with the part of ourselves which is largely hidden from us.

As we enter more fully into silence, we can begin to have the sense that, deep within us, God and our hearts are intimately entwined. God is so closely bound together with us that it sometimes seems difficult to distinguish God from our own hearts. God seems to be a part of our very being and to share our sense of who we are. There is what we may call a shared subjectivity. Yet, in all this, God is still distinct from us—intimately close, yet utterly separate. God remains God Almighty, to whom we relate with awe and reverence.

All this is possible because God is personal. Human beings derive their personal nature from God's personal nature. It is because we reflect God's personal being that we can enter a relationship with God, as between two people. So, when we enter the depths of ourselves in silent prayer, we encounter, not a being about whom we talk and think, but a personal presence, a 'You' who stands before us and confronts us.

Because this is a personal relationship, it is reciprocal. There is a give-and-take, a to-ing and fro-ing, between us and God. Strangely and wonderfully, in this relationship we do for God something of what God does for us. The Bible points to this by using many of the same words both of God and of us: God knows, holds, blesses, loves and is faithful to us, and we do the same for God.

The relationship is one of mutual sharing, but in each case it is God who takes the initiative. Just as we love because God first loved us, so all aspects of our relationship spring from the prior action and initiative of God. In the prayer of silence we engage in the give-and-take of this relationship, doing towards God what God is doing for us.

Among the many aspects of this give-and-take there are perhaps three aspects which find special expression in silent prayer. When we pray in this way we are deliberately seeking God, but we do so knowing that God is also seeking us. We wait for God, and know that God is patiently waiting for us. And in our silent waiting we offer or give ourselves to the God who has given and who goes on giving himself to us. All this is part of a mysterious and wonderful 'exchange' which takes place between us and God, and which adds a richness to prayer.

7.

Loving and Being Loved

TO PRAY IN SILENCE is to wait upon God in love. Silent prayer arises out of love for God, and reaches out to God's love for us. This is the unanimous view of the great writers on prayer and contemplation.

The gospel tells us that the first commandment is to love God with all we have—heart and soul and mind and strength; and that the second is to love our neighbour as ourselves. But love cannot simply be commanded. We cannot simply make ourselves love God and other people. Perhaps we need to remind ourselves that 'We love because He first loved us'.[16] God is love, and all love comes from God. The love we have for God is a response to God's love for us. So if we find that our love is cold, and our urge to the prayer of silence is weak, perhaps we need to focus more simply on God's love for us.

The phrase 'the love of God' can become too familiar, too routine, something we believe in as a part of our faith, and take for granted. The God of the Bible is not a cold and unfeeling God, but warm, and even passionate. God's love is not something abstract, an aspect of some official policy towards humankind, an article of faith. God doesn't just love each of us in a general way along with everyone else. God is 'my God', as the Psalmists say, and loves each of us in a deeply personal way, as someone who is unique and precious, to whom God has given life. God doesn't just love in a formal way, but wants us for himself; God has a heartfelt desire for us to be with him, as a mother wants a little child.

---

[16] 1 John 4: 19.

One of the basic elements of silent prayer is simply letting ourselves be loved. Perhaps this is part of the meaning of the saying of Jesus that we need to become like little children. In the stillness we can remind ourselves that God loves us unconditionally, now, just as we are. We can let ourselves be enfolded and wrapped in the love of God, letting God put his arms around us and hold us, enjoying the sense that God is pleased to have us with him.

To let ourselves be loved in this way is not self-indulgent or narrowly self-centred; it is the seed or source of our love for God and for other people. For as we sense that God loves and wants us just the way we are, we find ourselves warming towards God. It is out of this experience of being loved that our love for God grows. We cannot force it, or produce it by our own efforts: it grows and swells naturally, as we allow ourselves to be loved.

And it is from this that love of our neighbour grows. When I know that I am deeply loved by God, that I am precious and valuable to God just as I am, I realise that every other person is loved and valued by God in the same way. This is the source of a love for other people which makes no distinctions. Love of others, no matter who they are and what they are like, is a natural overflow from our sense of God's love for us. Isaac of Nineveh says:

> A person who has stillness and the converse of knowledge will easily and quickly arrive at love of God, and with the love of God he will draw close to perfect love of fellow human beings.[17]

---

[17] Isaac of Nineveh, *Discourses* I. 10: 33-34.

8.

Silent Adoration

THE PRAYER OF SILENCE has adoration as its centre. To adore is to focus on God alone. In the prayer of adoration we set aside all other ways of praying and all our other concerns, and concentrate for a little while simply on God and on nothing else. The English mystic writer Richard Rolle has said, 'God is that true joy which none can have who seek anything other than God.' Of course there are other things which we seek in other ways and at other times, but in the prayer of adoration, we seek only God. We engage, as Rolle says elsewhere, in 'meditations directed to God alone'.[18]

Adoration involves remembering before whom we stand. It is to acknowledge a transcendent presence, to hold ourselves before One who is 'greater than suns or stars', who dwells in light inapproachable. To adore is to be aware of the mystery and holiness of God, and to stand in reverence and humility before this mystery.

We can adore God in many ways. We can pour forth our adoration in songs and hymns of praise. We can express it in the words of liturgy or of poetry. Music can carry our adoration in a special way—whether resounding, soaring music that reaches towards heaven, or deeply hushed music that speaks of the mystery of holiness. But there is a sense in which the deepest adoration takes place in silence. Behind and beneath our highest words of praise and our most majestic music, there is a silence to which all words and music point. The worshippers in the Jewish Second Temple were summoned to worship with a call to silence: 'The Lord is in his holy temple, let all the earth keep silence before him.' Similarly, when we are aware of the presence of God in his

---

[18] *The Fire of Love*, Richard Rolle, Penguin Classics, pp. 115, 159.

mystery and holiness, our natural and appropriate response is to keep silence. All praise, according to St Ephrem the Syrian, moves 'from sound to silence'. The worship of heaven, he adds, is 'the silent praise of the angelic beings'. The person who loves God, says Rolle, 'praises God in song—but his song is in silence'. The prayer of silence is, in a very special way, a prayer of adoration.

It is true that in the prayer of silence we go down into ourselves, putting the mind into the heart and reaching towards our inmost self. From this it may seem as if silent prayer were a matter of concentrating on oneself. But we go down into the heart, not in order to be concerned with ourselves, but because the heart is the place where we are open to God and can focus on God alone. The place of adoration is our inmost self.

Nor is this silent adoration a world-denying or other-worldly thing. It is also part of the mystery of God that God is both the God of infinite majesty and transcendence, and also of tender compassion, faithful love, and deep concern for his creatures. As we focus on God alone, and make ourselves silent before God's holiness, we open ourselves to the outpouring of God's love, and to what God is doing, both within ourselves and in the world. From a deep awareness of the mystery of the God whom we adore arises a true concern for the world.

This silent adoration, even when it takes place in the solitude of our hearts, is never done alone. To pray in silence is to join the multitudes who ceaselessly engage in the silent worship of God. The sense of being part of this silent company hushes our minds and draws us deeper into adoration.

9.

Purity of Heart

SILENT PRAYER has much to do with purity of heart. Whoever wants to stand in God's holy place, says the Psalmist, must have clean hands and a pure heart. The Hebrew word for 'pure' means clear, empty and open. A pure heart is one that is clear, not cluttered up with all sorts of things, not filled with desires, distractions and things that demand attention; it is simple, swept clean, undivided in its focus and intention, dedicated and committed to God alone, preferring nothing to God. To be pure in heart is to be single-minded in our desire for God and our devotion to God. Purity of heart, said St Augustine, is an inner disposition of the heart which is focussed on God alone.

In order to engage in silent prayer we need a measure of this purity—some clean, clear, uncluttered space within us that is open to God. In the prayer of silence we aim to focus simply on God's being and presence. In our prayer we can bring all sorts of things to God—our thoughts and feelings, our plans, our failings, our thanks, our concern for others. But behind them all, as a basis for all our praying, there needs to be a silent concentration simply on God, for God's own sake, without attention to other things. To do this fully, we need purity of heart—a heart unencumbered by other things.

How, then, do we achieve purity of heart, or at least move towards it? Certainly it requires some effort on our part. We need to reduce our inner clutter, the thoughts and desires that pull us this way and that. We need to try to rid ourselves of what the early Fathers called 'evil thoughts' or 'passions'— that is to say, our secret selfish motives, our subtle ways of promoting ourselves and manipulating others, our hidden envy, resentment, superiority and judgment of others, and all the other things which distort our inner life, and which, on a larger scale, wreak havoc with the life of the world. We cannot do this by ourselves, but by acknowledging them and offering them to God, we can open a way for God to lead us towards purity of heart. This, like prayer itself, is a gift of God; we cannot produce it, but we can ask for it.

Purity of heart and silent prayer belong together, in that one enables the other. If we need a measure of purity of heart to engage in silent prayer, the converse is also true, that prayer itself leads to purity of heart. The continued practice of silent prayer is a means towards greater simplicity and purity of heart. Indeed, purity of heart can be said to be the aim of prayer. One of the great Desert Mothers suggests that prayer is a kind of holy incense that fumigates the heart and 'chases out foul patterns of thought', making the heart pure.

Thus at the deepest level the two become one: purity of heart is itself a kind of prayer. 'Purity of heart', says Aphrahat, one of the Syrian Fathers, 'constitutes prayer more than do all the prayers that are uttered out loud'.[19] When we stand before God with pure hearts, we are already engaged in a deep form of prayer.

Jesus said: 'Blessed are the pure in heart, for they will see God.'[20] In silent prayer we are looking towards God, directing the eyes of our heart towards God, and seeking the vision of God. In this life we see only through a glass, darkly, seeing only reflections in a mirror.[21] But if through silent prayer we reach towards greater purity of heart, in the end we shall see God face to face and be granted the perfect vision of God which is given to the pure in heart.

---

[19] *The Syriac Fathers on Prayer*, Sebastian Brock.
[20] Matt. 5: 8.
[21] cf. 1 Cor. 13: 12.

10.

God's Hiding Place

TO ENGAGE in silent prayer is to enter what Psalm 91 calls the 'secret place' or, more literally, 'the hiding place of the Most High'. There is within each of us a secret place, the inner chamber of our hearts, a place so secret that not only is it hidden from the world outside us, it is not even fully known to ourselves. It is a place known fully only to God. This is our secret place, but it is also God's hiding place, in a double sense.

It is the place where God hides himself. In the midst of our ordinary human life, God remains largely hidden. God hides in many ways, but for us God's most important hiding place is the human heart. If we want to be deeply in touch with God, we need to discover and enter this hiding place. We need to go down into our own place of inner private intimacy, where we are confronted by the mystery of our own being, which is where God hides. Even here God is not fully known, but here we can touch the hem of God's garment.

The hiding place of the Most High is also the place where God hides us. God takes us into his secret place and hides us there, in the shelter of God's presence. To engage in silent prayer is to let ourselves be hidden by God, to be gathered into the secrecy of God's hiding place, which becomes our hiding place. Here we are sheltered and protected. Here God keeps us safe, not from external troubles or even from mental distress, but from the power of evil to snatch or seduce us away from God, from the secret and hidden evils, the arrow that flies by day, the pestilence that stalks in darkness and the destruction that wastes at noonday.[22] In the intimacy of our shared hiding place, there is communion with God. Although

---

[22] cf. Psalm 91: 5-6.

God remains transcendent and beyond us, there is a mysterious closeness we do not usually know in any other way.

It is here, in this hiding place, that God's secret work of fashioning and moulding us takes place. Just as God mysteriously gave life to our personal being when we knew nothing of it, so now God shapes and forms our inner life in the depths of our hearts, working silently to transform and sometimes radically re-shape us, to conform us to God's own likeness. The prayer of silence is a means of opening ourselves to this work of God within his hiding place; a tool God uses in his secret workshop to change, renew and re-form us as he wills.

God's way in the world at large is also a hidden way. The deepest work of God, the most profound movement of God's Spirit in human lives, takes place in the unknown depths of people's hearts. The activity of God is like a seed germinating underground, or like leaven hidden in a loaf, unseen and unnoticed.[23] If we want to share in God's work in the world, we need to let it happen in secret, without it being obvious to the world. Of course, there is a place for external activity in the name of God, by word and deed. There are those who bear witness to the love of God by their words of challenge or comfort, and by their deeds of love and self-sacrifice. But those who adopt the way of silent prayer do God's work in other ways, by opening themselves to the secret activity of God within and around them. The contemplative way, the way of silent prayer, is a hidden way, often unnoticed amid the noise and activity of the world. It is the way of those who have let themselves be gathered into the hiding place of God, the way of those who dwell in the hiding place of the Most High.

---

[23] cf. Mark 4: 26-29; Matt. 13: 33.

11.

Prayer and Solitude

IT IS TRUE that when we pray we always do so with other people. Sometimes there are others round about and joining with us, and we are physically with them. But even when we are praying by ourselves and there is no one else about, we are still linked with others in our prayer.

Conversely, it is also true that when we pray in depth we always do so in solitude. Deep prayer comes from the heart, the place which no one else can enter, and where we are truly ourselves. There is a secret place within us, known only to God. In this deep place we are, and must be, totally alone, as far as other people are concerned. It is the place of inner solitude, where only God is present with us.

Inner solitude is not the same as being physically alone. People who live by themselves or are often on their own, and who may experience loneliness, do not necessarily enter their inner solitary place. Similarly, it is possible to go into one's inner solitude even when one is physically surrounded by others.

To enter deeply into prayer we need to cultivate our solitude. Jesus said: 'When you pray go into your inner chamber and shut the door and pray to your Father who is in secret.'[24] We all know the need to do this physically and literally at times, the importance of finding a quiet place, a private room, where we can be alone with God. People of silent prayer learn to cherish their times of physical aloneness. But the Eastern Fathers took this 'inner chamber' to refer also to the place of our inner solitude, the place where we are alone within ourselves. We need to go into this place

---

[24] Matt. 6: 6.

and 'shut the door'; shut out other thoughts and concerns, and focus solely on being alone with God.

This place of solitude can be a place of emptiness. There can be a spiritual loneliness, a feeling that others are not there in support, and that God is strangely remote. But in this place there can also be warmth and fullness, and a sense that the room is furnished with the rich tapestries of God. There can be awareness of the 'dizzying nearness of the Other', and of the communion of all the others who, wherever they are, are together with us, as they too enter their own place of solitude.

Among the ancient Eastern monks, there were some who lived as hermits in total solitude, and some who lived in communities with others. But some lived in what they called a 'lavra'. This was a collection of private cells, all in the same area, where each lived on his own, in solitude, alone with God, but knew that he was surrounded by the others as they all engaged together in entering their own solitude. In the depths of their aloneness there was a mysterious unseen togetherness.

This can be an image or a parable of the life of silent prayer. It is prayer done in the depth of our own solitude, but also in the mysterious company of others, in a kind of 'lavra'. Perhaps those of us who are brought together in an unseen way in our work of silent prayer, and who are prepared to explore the rich depths of our own aloneness with God, can have a sense that we form something of a hidden 'lavra' of this kind.

12.

Open to God

PRAYER need not be a matter of addressing God or expressing anything to God. It can be simply be a matter of opening ourselves to God's presence and to what God may be doing. Such prayer is based on the belief that God is active in hidden and unseen ways. God is at work through the Spirit in all sorts of places and situations; but the special place of God's operation is the human heart, which is our inner centre, our secret inner cave. It is the core of our personality, our inmost self, the place where I am 'Me'. It is a place that is unique to each of us, a secret place hidden to other people.

God is the hiding place of our inner being, where we are hidden and wrapped in God and where God is at work, silently and in hidden ways. Most of the time we do not know what God is doing within us, but we can to some extent make ourselves open to the secret operation of God. When in our silent prayer we go down into this inner place, we open ourselves to the God who works in our hearts. This is a part of the purpose of silent prayer.

This inner cave is not always easy to enter. It is partly hidden even from ourselves. It has depths that we ourselves do not know. Even what we can know of our own heart is to some degree covered over by ingrained ways of thinking and feeling, and by habitual attitudes. These we have unconsciously adopted to promote our superficial selves and protect ourselves from inner pain or emotional discomfort, and they obstruct the way to our inmost selves. In the prayer of silence, we try to go down below these protective layers into our heart, to reach as far as we can into our true inner selves, to enter our own secret place.

To do this we need to recognise, acknowledge and lay bare before God all that is going on in us; the thoughts and feelings that are with us or are affecting us as we come to pray, together with our plans, intentions, expectations, hopes and fears for the hours ahead. Having done this, we can then try to still our minds, gather together our wandering thoughts and calm our turbulent feelings, so that we can focus as much as possible on God alone.

In this way we open ourselves to the movement of God within us during our time of prayer. Prayer becomes not an attempt to address God, but a time when we make space for God's workings. Sometimes we can be very conscious that God is moving within us. We have a sense that something is happening, that we are being taken along, and we find ourselves in some way changed by our time of prayer. But often we may have no sense or feeling of what God is doing. This does not mean God is doing nothing, but that God is working in secret without our knowing it. And perhaps later we may find that we have been changed and turned round by what God has been doing.

This prayer of openness can then spill over into the rest of life. It can make us more able to discern the activity of God around us, and can result in our being more open to God's operations at other times, in other people and in other aspects of life. If we open our inner selves to God, this in a small way provides an opportunity for the actions of God in the world. Silent prayer becomes a means of co-operating and going along with the silent movements of God both within us and around us.

THE PRAYER OF SILENCE

II

RECEPTIVE WAITING

13.

Into Silence

UNDERLYING all our prayer there is silence. It is the basis of our relationship with God; through it we relate to God and God relates to us. Silence is a deep and incomprehensible mystery. It is not simply an absence of noise, but something real and positive. There are various kinds of silence, and we experience them in different ways. There is the silence of the world *around* us, which we can hear when the noise of the world dies away. There is silence deep *within* us, which we can sense beneath the clatter of our thoughts and the noisy distraction of our concerns, when we allow ourselves to be still and listen to our inner heart. And there is the silence *beneath* us—the silence that is part of the nature and being of God, an aspect of the ineffable mystery of the One who dwells in silence, infinitely beyond us yet intimately close within us. In the prayer of silence we reach down into silence.

Silence is at the heart of our relationship with God because it forms a deep means of communication. God communicates with us not only through words, but more profoundly and mysteriously through silence. God's message to us is expressed not only in verbal form, but through a movement of the heart, in ways we may not consciously recognize: through subtle nudges, inarticulate urges, or uninvited feelings. By holding ourselves still and silent before God we make ourselves open to these secret and unspoken movements within us. And we reciprocate, laying bare our inmost selves in God's presence, and opening up to God the secret feelings, motives, hopes and fears within us. It is this two-way communication, deeper than words, that forms the substance of our relationship with God.

Silent prayer doesn't mean prayer in which all thought ceases. We cannot stop the flow of our thoughts or prevent words forming in our minds. We should not try to empty our minds, but to focus our thoughts on God and to direct the unspoken words of our minds towards the things of God, perhaps using the words of a rhythm prayer. Isaac of Nineveh writes that pure contemplative prayer 'does not mean that the mind is entirely devoid of any thought or wandering of any kind, but that it does not wander about on empty subjects during the time of prayer'.[25] Silent prayer is not a closing down of our minds, but a reaching down towards the silence that underlies our minds.

When we pray in depth and sincerity, we enter into and make ourselves part of the mystery of silence. Silence is a sacramental reality, a part of ordinary life which can be a means of approaching God and of being united with God. Listening to the silence around us facilitates our entry into the silence within us, and this in turn enables us more easily to reach down to the silence beneath us: the rich, numinous silence which is a part of the very being of God.

Amidst the distractions of wandering thoughts and the concerns of daily life, we might touch the mystery of silence only occasionally. But, when we do, we can become aware of the reality of the warm love of God, silently accepting, embracing, enfolding and holding us. If we make a practice of approaching prayer in this way, we may find not only that silence becomes a greater reality for us, but also that some sense of silence may stay with us in the course of daily life. This is one of the fruits of the prayer of silence.

---

[25] Isaac of Nineveh, *Discourses* II. 15: 2.

14.

Waiting

WE ARE URGED by the Bible, and by the Psalms in particular, to 'wait for the Lord'. Waiting is at the heart of contemplative prayer and spirituality. To engage in silent prayer is to wait for God in emptiness and stillness.

How do we set about waiting for God? One way to begin is by offering or handing over to God all that is preoccupying us and filling our inner space: our thoughts and feelings, our desires and attachments, our wishes and fears, our plans and intentions. By clearing this inner space, we can make way for God.

It is from a sense of inner emptiness that desire for God arises. The vacant space within us is 'God-shaped'; it calls out to be filled with God. We know that without God we remain unfilled and empty—or filled only with artificial things. So the more we are aware of our emptiness, the more we long for God to fill it. It is this desire and longing that spurs our waiting. The only way to satisfy our longing for God is to wait for God.

To wait for God is to stay in our inner space in silence and stillness. It is an inner waiting, in which our spirit is not reaching for anything, not trying to achieve anything, not looking for progress in spiritual living, not working to overcome our faults, but simply being passive and still in spirit in order to allow the mysterious working of God to take place within us or through us. We cannot produce the presence of God, or regulate God's activity; we can only wait.

To wait for God is to wait with expectancy, but without expectation of anything in particular. In the well-known words of T. S. Eliot, it is to:

Wait without hope

For hope would be hope for the wrong thing.[26]

It is to open ourselves to the hidden, unseen presence and the secret, mysterious activity of God, which may be revealed in ways which we don't expect, or which may not be revealed at all. It is to wait in the dark, without any assurance that anything will appear. It is to wait only for God, for God's own sake, letting God be God in ways we do not understand and believing that God will use our waiting in his purpose for us and for the life around us.

Waiting for God is not only something we do in our times of silent prayer: it extends into the rest of life. If we learn to wait for the presence and activity of God in our times of silence, we find ourselves being open to this presence and activity in our daily living. Waiting can become a way of life in which we become more and more receptive and open to whatever God may be doing in the course of all the events of everyday life—in the disappointments and distresses as well as the joys.

There is no end to this waiting. While this life goes on, so does the waiting. Each time of deliberate silent prayer comes to an end, and we move on and do other things, but the waiting never ceases. In this life our longing for God is never fully satisfied, so we go on waiting in openness and hope, knowing that our waiting is used by God.

---

[26] *East Coker*, T. S. Eliot.

15.

Not-knowing-ness

ONE ASPECT of the prayer of silence is that it involves not knowing; being willing not to know.

In this kind of prayer we recognise that we do not know *how* to pray or *what* to pray for. Although we often pray for many things, there comes a point in our praying when we realise that we do not really know what we should pray for, because we do not know what is best or what God wants to give us. So we are content to remain in silence, and to wait for what God gives. Martin Luther put it this way:

> There are some who want to dictate the goal, manner, time and measure for God, and at the same time themselves suggest to him how they want him to help them. And if this does not come to them that way, they despair, or, if they can, seek help elsewhere. These do not have hope, they do not wait for God. ... But those who wait for God, they pray for grace, but they freely leave it to God's goodwill when, how, where, and by what means he will help them. About the help they do not despair; but they also do not give it a name. ... He who gives a name to the help will not receive it.[27]

If we do not know what to pray for, we have to recognise also that we do not really know *how* to pray either. We understand that prayer is not just a matter of words, but an attempt to reach out to God and be open to God; yet we do not fully know how to do this. As St Paul says, 'We do not know how to pray as we ought.'[28] We need the Spirit of God to enable us to be in touch with God, and so to engage in prayer in the fullest sense. Our silent prayer is the prayer of

---

[27] Martin Luther, WA 1. 208, quoted in Psalms 60-150.
[28] Rom. 8: 26.

not-knowing-ness, as we wait for God to bring about true prayer within us.

But there is more that we do not know. In the prayer of silence we recognise that we do not know the mystery of the workings of God. It is not just that God remains to a large extent unknowable and there is a 'cloud of unknowing' between us and God. It is also that we do not know what God is doing. The prayer of silence is made in the belief that God is indeed at work around us and in us, but most of the time God's activity cannot be seen and known. God works mainly in secret, and we cannot usually recognise what God is doing in the world and in people around us. Nor can we always discern God's workings within us. God works in hidden ways, deep within the heart, and the purpose of our silent prayer is to enable and give opportunity to this working. In opening ourselves quietly to God's hidden operation, we have to be content with not fully knowing what God is doing.

So the prayer of silence is the prayer of not-knowing-ness. It is, in the words of St John of the Cross, a 'travelling in darkness'. It is a matter of opening ourselves to the God whose 'paths are through the great waters', but whose 'footsteps are not seen'.[29] It is a prayer of deep and trustful quiet. Indeed, it is our very not-knowing-ness which calls forth our deep trust and enables the activity of God.

---

[29] Ps. 77: 19.

16.

Listening

IT IS OFTEN said that prayer is not only speaking but also listening. In the prayer of silence we make ourselves be still and listen to God. We stop our own talking in order to let God speak.

This is true, but it isn't always simple or easy. Listening is difficult and involves effort. It requires much more than external silence. Mother Mary Clare has written:

> Listening is a conscious, willed action, requiring alertness and vigilance. ... The obstacles to positive listening are numerous. Much of our time is spent talking and listening to ourselves. Our own voices are the chief obstacle to our listening either to God or to other people. ... It is not external noise but preoccupation with self which usually prevents us from listening. ... The external noises of the world are as nothing compared with the din we make within ourselves.[30]

If we are to listen to God, we need to silence this inner din and, as we all know, this requires practice and perseverance. Listening in a deep sense is not a skill that we acquire overnight but, if we are patient, what do we hear? In this, as in so many other things, people differ, and God's ways of dealing with us differ also.

There are some who, when they really listen, seem to hear God speak—not literally and physically, but in ways which make them feel that God is communicating with them. They can find themselves comforted, directed and challenged. This can be a rich experience, which gives a sense of the nearness of God, and can blossom into new ways of living and obedience. Listening can have this valuable reward. There are

---

[30] *Encountering the Depths*, Mother Mary Clare SLG, published by SLG Press, 1993, pp. 34-5.

dangers, of course, and we must be careful. In our listening we can sometimes hear the voice of our own dreams and fantasies, or of our over-socialized conscious and built-in sense of duty, or even the subtle insinuations of evil, and call it the voice of God. Nevertheless, there are some who, by a true and self-critical listening, can discern God's true utterance.

Others seem to be made differently. In spite of disciplined and open-hearted listening over long periods, they seem not to hear any voice or be able to discern any communication. Perhaps the explanation of this is that God's usual 'speech' is not directed to our conscious mind but to our inner hidden selves. God's 'converse' (to use an old-fashioned word) is with the secret heart. Listening, then, means 'listening in' to this converse, eavesdropping on the whispering of God to the heart, being aware that God is in communication with this deep inner self, though we may not know it. We may from time to time catch some echoes of this converse but, more often, we are just aware of a profound silence beneath which God is speaking in God's own secret way.

In the prayer of silence we rest content in the conviction that this converse is going on, and that God will maintain it; we go on listening whether we can overhear it or not, and may find ourselves agreeing with R. S. Thomas' rhetorical question:

Whose silence so eloquent
as his?[31]

---

[31] R. S. Thomas, *Collected Poems 1945-1990*.

17.

Prayer and Effort

THE PRAYER OF SILENCE is a calm, quiet waiting upon God. We know that God comes to us in God's own way and time. We do not make God come; what we do is wait. This may sound easy, but often it is not: it can be hard work. It is difficult to turn away from other things and focus our attention entirely on God. We have to make the effort of concentration.

So, does it all depend on our work and effort? Where does the grace of God come in? Doesn't our ability to pray depend on God who, by his grace, makes our praying possible? There is an inexplicable paradox here, which is well expressed by the Russian saint, Theophan the Recluse:

> Seek God: such is the unalterable rule for all spiritual advancement. Nothing comes without effort. The help of God is always ready and always near, but is only given to those who seek and work, and only to those seekers who, after putting all their powers to the test, then cry out with all their heart: Lord, Help us. So long as you hold on to even a little hope of achieving something by your own powers, the Lord does not interfere. It is as though he says; 'You hope to succeed by yourself—Very well, go on trying! But however long you try you will achieve nothing.' … You will achieve nothing by your own efforts; yet God will not give you anything unless you work with all your strength.[32]

It's not that we have to do it all ourselves; the ability to pray and the fruit of prayer come from the grace of God. But if we do not make an effort, we are clearly not serious in our desire for God, and God is unlikely to pour out grace and help.

---

[32] *The Art of Prayer: An Orthodox Anthology.*

Because prayer involves effort, we may find that we do not always *enjoy* our times of silent prayer. Waiting quietly for God is hard work and so it is not always enjoyable. We may even find sometimes that our waiting for God turns into waiting for the time of prayer to be over, so that we can get on with other things. Perhaps we can take comfort from the words of Julian of Norwich:

> Pray inwardly; though there seemeth to be no relish in it, yet it is profitable enough. Though thou shouldst feel naught, pray inwardly.[33]

Or, in a more modern translation: 'Pray inwardly, even if you do not enjoy it. It does good, though you feel nothing, see nothing.' Clearly even Julian found that she did not always enjoy, or 'relish', her inward prayer, but she was firmly convinced that it was 'profitable' nonetheless.

At times when prayer is a struggle and we are not especially enjoying it, we may question whether it is doing good. Such doubts should not concern us, because if our prayer is really focussed on God, for God's sake, we are offering it for God to take and use. Whether or not it does good then becomes a matter for God. Most of us find, thankfully, that our silent waiting for God does bear fruit within us, although it is not always apparent at the time. As we continue laying ourselves before God, we find ourselves more dependent on God. That, in Julian's words, 'is profitable enough'.

---

[33] *Revelations of Divine Love*, Julian of Norwich, Ch. 41.

18.

Emptiness

SILENT PRAYER involves being emptied. When we pray in depth, we seek to hand ourselves over to God, by offering up our thoughts and feelings and all that is in us. We are left empty and exposed before God. Here, in this silent place, where we are totally laid bare, we have to face our true selves. There can be no pretence, no avoidance; only the starkness of exposure, mixed with the comfort and assurance of knowing that we are accepted by God just as we are. Being ready to face our emptiness is part of the process of silent prayer.

Being emptied can mean even more than this. If we find ourselves stripped bare and naked, and are left standing alone and empty before God, we can be reminded that in reality we possess nothing. There is nothing that we can ultimately call our own—not our goods, our bodies or our minds. The very air we breathe is a gift from beyond us. We own nothing except our own inner selves—also given us by God. Here we know that everything on which we depend, or which we use to prop up our inner selves and boost our self-esteem, is transitory; that all the inner and outer empires we build are ephemeral and will one day dissolve. There is nothing of this world on which we can ultimately depend: we are totally dependent on God. This is a place where we are stripped bare of our defences. Here, to quote Mother Jane, we are 'despoiled of all protection, all spiritual and other props' and are 'nakedly exposed to God in a place that he calls prayer'.[34] This is a place of deep prayer.

There can be another kind of emptiness. We may, at times, find that our inner place of silence seems empty of God's reassuring presence, as if closed doors are keeping God

---

[34] Sister Jane SLG, *Loving God Whatever*, SLG Press, 2nd ed. 2008, p. 59.

from entering. In order to find God, we must go to a place where there is no God, and to which we cannot bring God by our own will. The kind of God who can be grasped by our thoughts or imagination, whom we can experience or envisage, just isn't there. There is only darkness and silence.

This is not a universal experience, but it does happen. If it does, all we can do is wait—wait silently in the dark, hoping that, although the doors are shut, God will somehow enter and be present for us. We may be rewarded with what seems like a glimpse of God, or a mysterious, intangible presence in the emptiness. We may even become aware of God coming to us, finding us, holding and embracing us, so that we find ourselves comforted and assured.

It may be, however, that God will not enter the place of emptiness in any discernible way. But even then we may realize, beneath the thoughts of our minds or the reach of our senses, that God is in fact there, within the apparent emptiness, hidden in the dark and inaudible in the silence. Our assurance then lies, not in any palpable sense of presence or glimpse of glory or whisper of God's voice, but in the deeper knowledge that our experience or awareness is not what matters. God can be real and present and active, even when we are unable to sense this or conceive of it. In the mystery of this deeper presence there is a more fundamental security; a hidden, immovable rock beneath our feet.

19.

Held by God

'YOUR RIGHT HAND holds me': so says Psalm 63. One way of approaching the prayer of silence is to remember that, in the deepest part of ourselves, God does hold us and keep us. It is not just something we hope for, or would like to happen; not something we need to strive after or try to bring about. It is not a matter of our asking God to hold us, or hoping that God will do so. It is a profound and mysterious reality, to which the Psalms, and other parts of the Bible, bear witness.

It is in our hearts that God holds us. Our inner selves, our true beings, are in the strong grip of God. This is vitally important for us in a number of ways. It means that God will keep us safe—not necessarily outwardly safe, protected from the hazards, misfortunes and tragedies of life, but inwardly safe. We can be secure in the knowledge that nothing can prise us from the hands of God; that no matter what may happen to us externally, our inner selves are safely held. Thus we are kept from being wholly taken over by evil. Evil does lay hold of us, of course, but God keeps us from falling and being lost. God does not allow us finally to separate ourselves off, rely on ourselves and go our own way. The things which come between us and God will not have the last word because God, by holding us, keeps us close to himself. Mysteriously, in the deep recesses of our hearts, God is present, and it is this presence that provides our ultimate safety.

It is probably true that most people don't experience God's hold upon them very vividly. Even if we engage lengthily and sincerely in silent prayer, waiting on God in stillness, we often do not have the sense of encountering God directly. But if we begin our prayer of silence by reminding ourselves that God holds us, and then attempt to reach down further into our hearts, we can find ourselves more aware of

God's holding. The sureness of God's grasp becomes not just an idea, but a conviction based on our own inner experience.

God holds us in a secret place which no one else can enter, and which is partly hidden even from ourselves. As we descend into our hearts, we find ourselves alone with God, closeted in secret with the God who mysteriously holds us in a place we cannot fully reach. In a way, of course, we are not alone. We are united in our silence with all others who, like us, are waiting quietly upon God: the great company of those who seek God. But to know something of God's hold on us, we must each go in solitude into that hidden centre of ourselves, and stand alone with God.

To do this is not to be exclusive or selfish, careless of other people and their needs. It is when we discover, in the secret depths of ourselves, something more of God's hold upon us, and know with full conviction that God keeps us, that we are able to be more truly ourselves. We can then be freed from some of the fears, anxieties, and self-promoting desires which distort our true being and separate us from other people.

It is the knowledge that God holds us, even when this is hard for us to discern, that enables us to remain before God in silent prayer. And it is by our silent prayer that we discover and deepen our sense of being held by God.

20.

Nothingness

WHEN WE engage in silent prayer, we turn our gaze inwards and we encounter a mystery. Deep within us, there is an area which is hidden from our conscious minds, something unknown, a kind of nothingness. To look deeply into ourselves is to face this nothingness and to realise that of ourselves we are nothing. Everything that we are or have is given to us, provided or enabled by God. God is our source and origin, from whom we have life, and it is only in God that we exist. Before God, we are something: each of us is a special being made in God's image. But without God we are nothing. Paradoxically, it is this nothingness that provides the basis of a deep relationship with God.

We all have some fear of nothingness, of non-being. So we try to cover it over, to hide from it, to pretend it isn't there. We run away from it by attaching ourselves to other things and clinging to them. We clothe ourselves, by our clinging, in order to cover our nakedness. We can do this in subtle ways, without realising it. We may inwardly cling to physical things: possessions, and material goods. But it is often our attachment to inner mental things that is more difficult to recognise and acknowledge: our plans and intentions, our ideas, our way of doing things, our sense of what is right and wrong; and, perhaps most subtle of all, our sense of who we are and the kind of person we are. We need all these things, of course, and having them is not wrong. The trouble arises when we become attached to them, when we are afraid of losing them or having them changed. We can find ourselves, perhaps unconsciously, clinging to them as a way of escaping from the nothingness we secretly fear, of hiding from our own nakedness.

To find our true life in God, and to be the person God intends us to be, we need to begin to give up our attachment to the things of this life. We can do this by entering deeply into silent prayer. Standing silently before God helps us to be aware of the hidden things we cling to. By opening and offering to God these hidden attachments, we can begin to loosen our hold on them. We don't give up all material things or abandon the mental structures which are a part of our life, but we aim to let go of our attachment to them, to stop clinging to them and to cling only to God.

To stand before God in silent prayer is to let ourselves be nothing, to enter our own nothingness. Here, we are stripped of all that usually supports us and gives us external reassurance, and we have nothing to hold onto but God. It is a kind of dying—a preparation for the physical death we must all undergo, in which we must abandon all earthly attachments.

Confronting our nothingness is not easy or comfortable, but it is when we are naked, without the protection of earthly attachments, that we truly find God. For here we discover that God holds us in our nothingness. In the words of the Psalm, 'My soul clings to you, and your right hand holds me.'[35] Our hold on God may not be very sure, but it is the experience of countless people that when, through our silent prayer, we give up clinging to other things and cling only to God, then God's hand does indeed hold us fast.

---

[35] Ps. 63: 8.

21.

When God Seems Absent

THE PRAYER OF SILENCE is a matter of holding ourselves still in the presence of God. But people who engage in this kind of prayer know that God is not always experienced as present. To borrow a phrase from the Psalms, God sometimes 'hides his face'. From time to time, and sometimes for no discernible reason, God does not seem to be available and present for us.

Sometimes the feeling that God is absent is particularly acute. One can be overwhelmed by a sense of darkness or emptiness, when God seems distant and prayer becomes impossible. The early monks and contemplatives knew times like these; Isaac of Nineveh describes the experience and offers advice to fellow monks:

> Let us not be perturbed if we are in darkness. I mean that special darkness in which the soul languishes at times and is, as it were, among the waves; and whether a man reads the Scriptures, or practises his rule, in whatever he does darkness follows upon darkness. He leaves his work, and very often is even unable to go near it. That hour is full of despair and fear; hope in God and the comfort of faith in Him are completely lost by the soul, and the whole of it is filled with doubt and fear. But God does not abandon the soul in such a state for long, and soon makes a way to escape. But I will tell you, and give you this advice: if you have no strength to master yourself and to prostrate yourself in prayer, then wrap your head in your cloak and sleep, until the hour of darkness is over, but do not leave your cell.[36]

Such times have been known throughout the years to those who have waited for God's presence. Isaac's words can be set alongside the much later description by St John of the Cross

---

[36] Isaac of Nineveh, *Discourses* I, 50.

of the 'dark night' experienced by many who follow a spiritual path:

> God turns all this light of theirs into darkness, and shuts against them the door and the source of the sweet spiritual water which they were tasting in God. ... And thus he leaves them so completely in the dark that they know not whither to go with their sensible imagination and meditation; for they cannot advance a step in meditation, as they were wont to do aforetime, their inward senses being submerged in this night.[37]

Sometimes, it is true, the cause of this kind of darkness can be found within ourselves, and an honest searching of our own soul will reveal what it is that separates us from God. According to the Old Testament prophets, God sometimes hides his face because of human sin. On the other hand, many people share the experience of the psalmists, who found these times of God's absence inexplicable. God withdraws and darkness descends for no apparent reason, and no amount of seeking or attempted prayer brings God's return.

In such circumstances, there is nothing we can do but wait. This is the meaning of Isaac's advice to his fellow monks, to wrap their heads in their cloaks and sleep, but not to leave their cells. Many have found that waiting quietly and in hope has eventually brought them nearer to God and more aware of God's presence. Indeed, times of darkness, or the apparent absence of God, can be seen as normal parts of the process by which we are led closer to God. St John of the Cross saw the 'dark night' as a 'recurring crisis along the spiritual path'. The hiding of God's face, although experienced as something negative, can in reality be a part of God's mysterious activity. Encountering the darkness of God's absence is, for many people, an important element in the deepening of faith.

---

[37] *Dark Night of the Soul,* St John of the Cross, Complete Works vol. 1, trans. E. Allison Peers, I. 8: 3, p.372.

22.

Divine Darkness

TO PRAY IN SILENCE is to enter the dark. The Bible says that God is light, but it also pictures God as dwelling or hiding in darkness.[38] There is a mysterious darkness surrounding God. This is not the darkness of evil, nor the darkness of pain, grief or depression, but what is often called the 'divine darkness'. All the great mystics in both east and west speak of this. Gregory of Nyssa says that in deep contemplation a person 'is cut off on all sides by the divine darkness'. Isaac of Nineveh speaks of 'the dark cloud of God's glory'. Walter Hilton says that the desire for God leads us into a 'luminous' and 'profitable darkness'. John of the Cross writes of the different kinds of 'dark night'. And Thomas Merton tells how the call of God 'plunges us into darkness and silence'.

So what is this divine darkness? It is first a darkness that lies between us and God. For us God is not visible. 'No one has ever seen God.'[39] God is beyond our thoughts and our imagining. Our minds cannot reach or grasp God; our language cannot define or describe God. There is a 'cloud of unknowing', an area of darkness, that comes between us and God. When we engage in silent prayer, we can be aware that we are entering this area of darkness. Usually we shut our eyes, to exclude the light and all things visible, and we can then focus our closed eyes and gaze into the dark. But no matter how long we gaze, or how deeply we are drawn into the divine darkness, God does not make himself obvious to us. We cannot penetrate through the darkness and bring ourselves face to face with God, but must simply continue to pray in silence and wait for God.

---

[38] Ps. 18: 11.
[39] John. 1: 18.

There is another, more mysterious kind of darkness, the darkness of God himself. In the well-known words of Henry Vaughan, 'There is in God, some say, a deep but dazzling darkness.'[40] The light of God is so bright, according to some, that when we gaze towards it our eyes are blinded, and we can see only the dark. God for us is dark because 'the awesomeness of the divine essence is more than human nature can endure'.[41] The darkness of God represents the unfathomable mystery, the unknown depth, the invisible wonder of God. Before this mysterious darkness, our spirits are hushed into silence and our heads are bowed in adoration and wonder. In the prayer of silence we hold ourselves still before the mystery of the deep but dazzling darkness of God.

Although the divine darkness may prevent us from grasping God, or knowing God with our minds, we can be given what one might call a sense of presence. We can become aware that the darkness is not totally empty, that in some mysterious way we are accompanied, that the darkness is 'dazzling', or vibrant, or filled with God. For us, as for Gregory of Nyssa, the dark can be 'truly an experience of the presence of God'.[42] We cannot know God with our minds but, in the dark, we can know God with the knowledge of the heart. We cannot see God with our eyes, but the dark can be bright with God's presence. To walk in the dark is to walk by faith and not by sight, with doubts, with uncertainties, with no proof of God and no clear map of the road ahead. It is to walk under a sky which is a night sky, yet one glistening with the stars of the mysterious presence of God. T. S. Eliot wrote, 'I said to my soul, be still, and let the dark come upon you, which shall be the darkness of God.'[43] If in the stillness of silent prayer we let the dark come upon us, we can discover that it is indeed the darkness of God.

---

[40] *The Night*, Henry Vaughan, 1650-5.
[41] *From Glory to Glory: Texts from Gregory of Nyssa's Mystical Writings*, Jean Daniélou, Introduction.
[42] *Ibid.*
[43] *East Coker*, T. S. Eliot.

THE PRAYER OF SILENCE

III

RESPONDING TO GOD

23.

God Acts First

OUR RELATIONSHIP with God in prayer is reciprocal, but God leads the way. All that we do is in response to what God does first. This points to at least three things which can be of help in silent prayer.

First, God waits for us before we wait for God. We often speak of silent prayer in terms of waiting for the Lord, but we sometimes forget that before we start consciously to wait for God, God is waiting for us. 'The Lord waits to be gracious to you',[44] says Isaiah. The realisation that God is there waiting for us can be a great encouragement and incentive to prayer, particularly on those occasions when prayer does not come easily. We may be distracted and unable to focus on God, or God may seem absent, but God is there, waiting for us, more ready to hear than we are to pray. God is with us, even if we do not feel we are with God.

Secondly, God wants us before we want God. God's love for us is not an abstract thing, but a warm desire and affection. God wants us to be with him and it is above all for this reason that we come to God in prayer. One of the most basic aspects of prayer, especially the prayer of silence, is simply letting God want us. It is a matter of letting ourselves be loved just as we are; of accepting, enjoying, even indulging ourselves in God's love for us. This is not all there is to prayer, but it is a fundamental element. God wants us, not because we are good and obedient, but simply because each of us is unique; a precious person whom God has made for himself. We can, for a while, forget our obligations and anxieties, and the things we feel we ought to be doing in our

---

[44] Isa. 30: 18.

prayer, and just let ourselves go into the love of God, and be loved. If it is true, as we say, that God loves us just as we are, we need to give God opportunity to do so—the chance to put his arms round us. In our attempts to do and be what we think God wants, we sometimes forget that what God wants most of all is to love us. The prayer of silence is, in part at least, a matter of accepting and enjoying the extraordinary warmth and affection of God's desire for us.

Thirdly, God's hold on us is stronger than our hold on God. The psalmist says, 'My soul clings to you and your right hand holds me'.[45] In our prayer of silent waiting we cling, or cleave, to God; but there is inevitably something tentative and unsure about it. We cannot be totally sure of our hold upon God: from time to time it slips. As we engage in silent prayer we renew our hold on God, but our prayer gets distracted, and our focus becomes blurred. Our prayer is only possible because, all the time, whatever our prayer is like, God's hold on us is sure. We may cling tentatively, but God holds us firmly and securely, in the deepest part of ourselves.

In this relationship, God waits for us and we wait for God; God wants us and we want God; God holds onto us and we cling to God. In each case, what we do stems from, and is the result of, what God does first. Silent prayer involves entering into, enjoying, and feeling secure in what God does for us; being still and remembering that God is waiting for us, letting ourselves be wanted and loved, and held in the grip of God.

---

[45] Ps. 63: 8.

54

24.

Wonder

TO ENGAGE in silent prayer is to open ourselves to wonder. In our prayer we find ourselves facing what may seem like two contradictory realities. On the one hand God is an incomprehensible and immense mystery. God cannot be imagined in our hearts, or understood by our minds, or described in our words. Silent prayer involves placing ourselves before the immeasurable, infinite and everlasting majesty and mystery of God. In the deep silence of prayer we recognise that our lives are lived out under the wonder of the over-arching canopy of this incomprehensible mystery.

Before this wonder, we can find that our spirits are hushed into silence and our minds stilled into reverence. Before this wonder, we can be drawn to bow our heads or to bend our knees, or perhaps even to prostrate ourselves to the ground. Before this wonder, we can recognise and acknowledge our insignificance, our smallness and the transience of our being. We are humbled before the mystery and majesty of God. This is a fundamental aspect of silent prayer. To forget this is to try to reduce God to our own dimensions; to make God containable within our own minds. To engage in silent prayer is to be still before the wonder of this mystery.

But there is an even greater wonder: that this infinite and unattainable God is also intimately close to us; so close that God can be said to be in us, and we in God. Silent prayer is a matter of recognising this closeness, of seeking to be in God, and of allowing ourselves to be drawn deeper and deeper into God. We wait in silence in the ante-chamber of our hearts until God takes hold of the centre of our being and wraps us in himself.

To be drawn completely into God in this way is, no doubt, something that happens only for mystics or for a few; but it can happen to some extent for anyone who engages in silent prayer. We may sometimes find that God comes so close to us, and we to God, that God seems closer to us than we are to ourselves. We may have a sense that God lives in us, shares our thoughts and actions, rejoices and weeps with us; and that we, for our part, live and move and have our being in God. We know then that our good deeds, our holy and humble thoughts, our feelings of love and kindness, are all the gift of God; and so, in our silent prayer, we open ourselves to God's grace and offer our own thoughts and actions in cooperation with the activity of God. We discover that prayer is a double activity, that God prays in us and we pray in God; that our very desire to pray, while it is our own and comes from within us, is also the gift of God. And so prayer becomes, not an exchange of messages with a distant being, but an intimate encounter. This is the wonder of God's closeness to us.

In the depth of prayer, these two truths of God come together. This can be said not only of mystics: it can be true in some measure of all of us. As we pray in silence we can be aware that the God who is so intimately close to us is also the God of mystery and majesty whose dwelling is beyond the stars; that the God who is unreachably beyond us is also to be encountered deep within us. We can find ourselves mysteriously stretched between the God of infinite majesty and the God of intimate closeness. When this happens we know something of the wonder of prayer.

25.

God's Process

IN SILENT PRAYER we seek to acknowledge and cooperate with God's process. Our life—our own unique, inner personal life—is a gift from God. Having brought us into being for a purpose, God continues to work within us to fulfil and complete that purpose. Through external influences and the events which take place in our own hearts and minds, God continues to mould us into what we were intended to be. Our sense or knowledge of God, our relationship with God, our longing for God and our urge to pray is all the result of this process. Whatever degree of faith, hope and love there may be in us, it has been planted there, not by our own actions or intentions, but by God. Through all the ups and downs of life, God leads us towards our true home

Our part is to be open to this process, to make space for the working of God within us throughout our lives, and to allow and cooperate with what God is doing. Living a spiritual life is not a matter of making ourselves more godly or more spiritual; it is not primarily a matter of doing God's will, but of allowing and encouraging God's process within us.

This is a part of the purpose of silent prayer. As we make ourselves still and silent before God, we are opening up and making ourselves available for the operation of God's process within us. Silence can make us more sensitive to the delicate nudges and often inaudible whispers by which God furthers this purpose within us.

We can, of course, obstruct God's process. We can very easily become so centred on ourselves that we are unresponsive to God's activity within us. There may be times when it is hard to recognise and believe that God is indeed active within us; when God seems to have abandoned us, or when our own wilfulness seems to have made God despair of us. But God is persistent and determined; not so easily thrown off. We can be assured and confident that the God who has a purpose for us and has planted a desire for God within us, the God to whom we have begun—however inadequately and falteringly—to respond, will not rest until the process is complete, and we belong wholly to God. Amidst all the ups and downs and inadequacies of our attempts at prayer and spiritual living, this can be a source of comfort.

When, as individuals, we understand that God is at work within us, we can recognise that God has a purpose for and is at work within everyone, albeit sometimes in hidden ways; even in people whom we may dislike or despise, even in those who are responsible for terrible and wicked acts. Knowing this can give us a new way of regarding other people, and can become for us the source of a tender and inclusive intercession, embracing even the most unlikely-seeming people. In this way our silent prayer can become a channel for the operation of God's purpose, not only within ourselves, but within others as well.

26.

Receiving

TO ENGAGE in silent or contemplative prayer is to make ourselves ready to receive. We are often urged to give, and giving is indeed an important part of Christian living; but along with giving goes receiving. A contemplative relationship with God is one in which we are always ready to receive.

Receiving is not simply taking, and it is more than just accepting. One can accept unpleasant facts or situations with resignation, just as one can politely accept an unwanted gift. But receiving is different from that. It involves an attitude of mind that takes something positive from whatever we are given or confronted with. It is a way of taking a proffered gift into ourselves and welcoming it; of seeing in every situation something to be valued.

Receiving is part of the nature of God. We offer God our worship, our praise, our thanks, and our whole life, and God receives all this with graciousness, with courtesy and with care. It is a thing of wonder that Almighty God, Creator of heaven and earth, welcomes and takes pleasure in the little gifts that each of us offers. The Almighty Giver is also the Great Receiver, and it is God who gives us the gift and grace of receiving. As God receives what we give to him, so we receive what God gives to us. In drawing closer to God we too can grow in the grace of receiving.

We can receive from God in many ways. One way is through silent prayer itself. By being still in God's presence, we are making ourselves ready to receive things that may come to us without our expecting or even being aware of them. In our silence there may come thoughts, feelings or intuitions that God plants in us. Or God may gently nudge us in a certain direction, or silently offer us encouragement or hope. A time of inner silence before God enables us to receive all these things and take them to ourselves. Of course, such things do not always come to us during prayer. But to pray in silence is to make ourselves available to receive the thoughts and realizations that may come, and the hidden activity of God within us.

We can also receive through things that happen to us. When pleasant and enjoyable things happen, we can learn not only to accept them but to receive them as gifts of God. We can also receive from unpleasant, difficult or painful things. Naturally, we try to alter or avoid these things when they occur, but if we can't, we have to accept them, and we can also learn to receive from them. By looking for what God may be doing or saying through them, we can receive a gift from God. By being ready, through silence before God, to receive from an intractable situation, we may find that it is transformed or transfigured, so that we are enabled not only to accept it, but to find within it something to be welcomed and valued. We can be shown a way which lies between resistance and passive acceptance; a way of inner receptiveness.

Our relationship with God is always one of receiving as well as giving. It is by receiving that we learn truly to give. The way of silent prayer is a way of growing in this grace of receiving.

27.

Water from the Rocks

SPIRITUALITY is not so much a matter of how we say our prayers as of how we respond to what is given us in life. No doubt it is important to try to find times when we can escape from activity and noise and demands and settle into a period of deep, uninterrupted silence before God; and it is very helpful if we can establish a pattern for doing this. But sometimes our attempts seem repeatedly to be frustrated. Even if we try very hard to reduce our activities and cut out some of the things which take up our time, many important things seem to remain which demand our attention, and make regular or lengthy periods of silent prayer difficult to attain. More than that, sometimes troubles and distressing problems weigh upon us so heavily that they fill our minds, and stifle our search for silence and peace.

How can we follow the path of silent prayer in the midst of all this? Faced with these difficulties, we may find ourselves feeling guilty, blaming ourselves for our lack of discipline and our neglect of serious prayer. We may feel that we ought to try harder and do better. Or perhaps that we should just give up and acknowledge that silent prayer is 'not our thing'.

Perhaps we need to think of prayer not as something separate from ordinary life, for which we need to escape from everyday things for a while, but as a means of offering this life to God. Of course it is good to have the opportunity to do this in a long period of peaceful and uninterrupted silence, and it is important to try and find such opportunities. Often, however, it is a matter of doing it in the midst of the activities and demands of life; of finding a few minutes at certain times deliberately to go down into inner prayer; or of pausing from time to time in the midst of our activity to offer it all to God.

It is also important not just to offer our ordinary life to God, but to be able to look for God in the midst of it. It may be relatively easy to do this when life is pleasant and enjoyable and things are going well. We can recognise the goodness of God amongst the good things of life. Recognising the hand of God amongst the boredom of everyday living, or amongst the hard and frustrating things that afflict us is more difficult. A truly spiritual and Christian way of life is not a matter of always trying to avoid difficulties and frustrations, but of trying to discover what God is doing and saying to us through them; not of finding ways of bypassing the rocks and hard places, but of discovering how to draw refreshing water from the rocks.

This is difficult, and many of us are not very good at it. We regard even minor frustrations as things which shouldn't happen. More serious anxieties, pains and problems tend to blow us off course altogether and get in the way of our life of prayer. But we have probably all known some truly saintly people, who have been able to accept the 'slings and arrows of outrageous fortune' not just with resigned equanimity but as sources of spiritual nourishment.

We can't learn to do this quickly and easily. Perhaps, though, if we make a practice of trying, in a small way, to see more and more of ordinary life in the light of God, and of offering as much of it as we can to God, we may become more aware of God's hand in it. Even if we don't, the practice of focussing ever more single-mindedly on God, and of going deeper and deeper into God in silent prayer, may make us more able to trust that God is at work even when his hand is unseen. Even without knowing it we may be given water from the rocks.

28.

Pour Out Your Hearts

'POUR OUT your heart before God',[46] says the Psalmist. This is a good way of describing one approach to prayer, and to contemplative prayer in particular.

In referring to the 'heart' we often mean our feelings. When we are beset by troubles or distress it can be comforting to tell someone else how we feel, to share our emotional turmoil, to pour out our hearts to another person. It naturally follows that we should want to open and lay before God our feelings of distress. But we can uncover other feelings too: pleasure, anxiety, unease—the often superficial emotions that are affecting us at the time of prayer. We can also reach down and expose to God the deeper currents of feeling that are flowing within us, which may be partly hidden from us most of the time. To do this is to pour out our hearts before God, and this is one important aspect of praying.

The heart in the biblical sense, however, is not just the place of feeling and emotion; it is also the place of thought and decision-making. So, in our prayer, we can place before God whatever is going on in our minds—the thoughts which preoccupy us, the issues which concern us, our intentions and expectations, and whatever decisions we have made or are still pondering. This is another important way in which we can pour out our hearts in prayer.

In the Bible, the heart has another meaning beyond this. It is the core of our being, the secret identity that is mysteriously embedded within each of us. In prayer we can

---

[46] Ps. 62: 8.

recall this essential inner self which God has made and given us; which comes from God, will return to God, and has no existence apart from God. When we pour out our heart, we lay bare our inner self before God.

In spreading out before God our feelings and emotions, our thoughts, intentions and decisions, and all that is at the core of our being, we are emptying ourselves, and so we are left inwardly vacant, a shell. Of course this doesn't happen for us completely or perfectly. For most of us, our outpouring is half-hearted and partial, impaired by distractions; but however incomplete, it can be a way into contemplative prayer.

In the prayer of silence we stay quietly for a while in this place of emptiness, waiting for God to fill it. We may sometimes be aware of being filled by the rich presence of God, of the Holy Spirit being poured into our hearts to replenish and restore our empty space. Probably this is not something we experience often; but what we may more frequently receive is a sense that our feelings, our thoughts and our inner self, which we have poured out, are being given back to us afresh, returned to us purified by God's acceptance. And with this sense we can move on strengthened and reassured.

Whatever happens or does not happen when we pour out our hearts to God, contemplative prayer involves a willingness to remain for a short time with the empty vessel of ourselves, with our hands open and outstretched, waiting for whatever God may give to fill us.

29.

Here Am I

ONE WAY of beginning a time of silent prayer is to repeat the words 'Here am I', or 'Here I am'. This simple phrase, found frequently in the Bible, can be used to express our response to the invitation of God, and to lead us into the prayer of silence.

In the Old Testament, the phrase is used to translate a Hebrew word which means, literally, 'Behold me!' When I say 'Here am I', I am asking God to behold me. I am consciously placing myself in the sight of God, inviting God's attention and scrutiny; a scrutiny which is searching but also accepting, compassionate and loving. In silent prayer we allow ourselves to linger within the sight of God, consciously aware that God is looking at and paying attention to us. To say 'Here am I' is to know the wonder of receiving God's personal attention.

To say 'Here am I' is to acknowledge that the one who comes before God is none other than 'I' or 'Me', the unique being whom God has created. In the words of the old 'spiritual', 'It's Me, it's Me, O Lord; not my father nor my mother but it's Me, O Lord.' It's Me, my true inner self, standing before You with as much honesty as I can muster, without pretence and quite defenceless; it's Me, with all that is within me, good and bad, present before You. Here am I, with my secret self laid open and bare before God.

To say 'Here am I' is also to acknowledge that I am alone with God. Whatever my outward physical surroundings may be, inwardly there is no one else present. Of course, even at this time of solitude, I am one of a large company of those who stand before God. I am supported by the knowledge that there are countless others, known and unknown, who are alone with God in their own place of inner solitude. It is also true that, whilst I am in solitude with God, I am still part of this world, sharing in the woes and the wonders of life along with all humanity. Nevertheless, when I say 'Here I am', for the moment there is no one inwardly present besides me and my Maker, my Father-and-Mother God, the source and origin of my being. And, wonderfully, to be alone with God is to discover anew that God, in love and graciousness, is willing to be alone with me.

'Here am I' is, in addition, a response to a summons or a call. It expresses a readiness to serve, to listen and obey; a willingness to be directed by God. God's direction does not usually come in the form of explicit commands, or clear messages telling us what to do, or what God's will is. More often it is expressed through quiet promptings, or through the secret, silent movement of God within ourselves, of which we may not even be aware. When I say 'Here I am', I am declaring my willingness to listen for and to try to discern and attend to these inner promptings. I am opening myself to this quiet operation of God within me.

'Here am I' is our response to the call of God; but, wonderfully, it is also God's response to us. We can come to God saying 'Here am I' because God does the same for us. 'You shall call', says Isaiah, 'and the Lord will answer; you shall cry, and he will say, Here I am'.[47] It is because God first says 'Here am I' to us, that we are moved to come to God saying 'Here am I'; 'Behold me'.

---

[47] Isa. 58: 9.

30.

Feelings and Prayer

WHAT do we do with our feelings when we try to pray in silence? Many people find that feelings get in the way and prevent them from concentrating on prayer as they would wish. We can be affected by feelings of various kinds— troublesome feelings of anxiety, sadness, resentment or anger, or pleasurable feelings of excitement, anticipation or hope— and these can take us over, disturb our silence and swamp our prayer.

Such feelings may not be in the forefront of our consciousness. They may be latent and tucked away, yet powerful enough to be a disturbance to our inner selves, perhaps even without our knowing it. Our prayer can be blocked by feelings of which we are scarcely aware.

There is a school of thought which maintains that prayer is not about feeling, and that to pray properly we should suppress our feelings by making greater effort to concentrate on God alone. If the feelings concerned are slight or trivial, this is probably right. A little determination, perhaps with the use of a rhythm prayer, will enable us to keep our focus on God. But if the feelings are strong and deep-seated, we probably find that we can't avoid them. It is no good telling ourselves that we shouldn't feel like this, because feelings such as these cannot be dismissed.

So what can we do? One approach is to adopt the formula 'acknowledge and offer'. The first step is to recognize, acknowledge and admit our feelings. This may not be as easy as it sounds. If our feelings are deep-seated, tucked away and hidden, it may take some time and a certain amount of self-searching before we can see and own what it is that we are feeling. If our feelings are ones which we don't want to have, or which we think we shouldn't have, it can be humiliating to acknowledge them even to ourselves. But whether they are deep-seated or more superficial feelings, we must, first of all, recognize and own them for what they are, good or bad, and acknowledge in honesty, both to ourselves and to God, what is going on within us.

This may include an acknowledgement that our feelings are mixed, jumbled and contradictory. They are not logically consistent. Some of the Psalms express different and apparently contradictory feelings in the course of one poem, which is often regarded as a problem by those who look for rational consistency. But these Psalms can be seen as a true and honest expression of the fact that we often feel different things at the same time; and this, in turn, may help us to recognize and acknowledge our own jumbled feelings.

The second step is simply to offer all our feelings to God, whatever they are. This is not the same as 'letting them go'. It is often not possible just to 'let go' of strong or deep-seated feelings. Offering is a matter of handing over or giving them to God in such a way that, although they are still with us, they are opened to God. God is invited to take, use, transform and sanctify them. Here, too, the Psalms can be of help. They give us words to express and hand over these varied feelings to God, demonstrating that everything, including all kinds of feelings, can form an offering. Sometimes a psalm expresses apparently contradictory feelings, but as Robert Davidson points out in his commentary on the Psalms, both types of feelings are thereby offered to God.

31.

What God Made Us to Be

EACH human person is a unique creation of God, designed to fill a particular place in God's scheme of things. God has made each of us for himself, to be something special and precious for God, a jewel, a polished stone in God's crown. Each of us has a unique and irrevocable vocation to become the person that God has made us to be. And it is a part of the purpose of life to discover and be that person.

Engaging in silent prayer is one way of trying to be the person we actually are now. We all know that being that person does not always come naturally. Our true self is often hidden beneath superficial layers of thought and behaviour, and perhaps of self-deception. We can create a false image of the kind of person we think we are and then try to live up to that image. But when we hold ourselves silently and openly in the presence of God we are confronted with the person we truly are. Here there can be no pretence, no escaping from the reality of ourselves.

So the practice of silent prayer is a voyage of discovery into our own nature. In silent prayer we go down into our own depths, reaching as far as we can into our inner selves, and directing our attention to God who is deep within us. As we continue in it we discover more about the kind of person we are within ourselves. Sometimes this can be unsettling, even painful. But, as we silently remember the presence of God, we discover also that God accepts us as we are; that God loves, not the person we think we are or would like to be or try to be, but the person we really are. This realisation that we don't need to change or be different for God to accept and receive us, makes it easier for us to accept ourselves as we are.

And, paradoxically, it is by accepting ourselves as we are that we open the way for God to change us, and to bring us more into line with God's intention for us. By our silent prayer we open ourselves to the action of God to change and transform us. We empty ourselves of the things that prevent God's activity, pouring out before God our inner attachments and standing before God in emptiness and nothingness. This allows God to remould and reshape us, to refine and polish us, to remake us according to God's likeness, and gradually to transform us into what God designed us to be.

This sense that we are being shaped into what God originally intended can provide deep satisfaction, and a sense of purpose and fulfilment. And, more than that, it can also make us aware that God has made every other person with a special purpose also, that there is something special for everyone to be. This applies to all—to the good and the bad, the likeable and the unlikeable, those who are important in the world's eyes and those who are insignificant—all are made to be jewels in God's crown, each with her or his special place. When we see that God is working to transform each person into who he or she was meant to be, we find ourselves more able to accept, respect, and even love, people of all kinds.

Silent prayer is a way of allowing God, through his mysterious, transforming work in us, to make us into what God intended us to be, to complete the purpose God has for us, and to lead us home.

32.

Contemplative Living

THE WORD 'contemplative' is often applied to prayer. But it can be used not only of prayer but of life itself. We can aim to be contemplatives in our way of living. The contemplative life can be described as one that is characterised by an attitude of receptivity and acceptance, both in our praying and in our daily living.

Contemplative prayer is receptive prayer. In this way of praying we hold ourselves still before God and wait for what God has to give us. It is not a matter of telling God what we want, but of allowing God to give us what he wants. There is, of course, a place for making our desires known to God; but in silent prayer we move beyond that into a simple readiness to receive. This requires an opening of our inner emptiness to receive God and what God is doing; a clearing out of the thoughts that are cluttering our inner selves, to make space for whatever God may give, whether during the time of our praying or in the course of our life in the coming hours and days.

Contemplative prayer gives birth to the contemplative life. Through this prayer we can be made into contemplative people, which means being open to what comes; being ready to perceive God in whatever is happening to us and around us, and to receive whatever God may give us through what is happening. The events and situations that confront us bring us something of God. Some of them call us to penitence, some require our patience, and some evoke our compassion. Even the dark, unpleasant things show signs of God's hand. In all things we can look for some token of God's presence or some beckoning of God's hand. Contemplatives are open to perceiving and receiving these things because their souls have been stilled in the silence of prayer. Contemplative living means accepting what happens around us as things through which God is acting or speaking. It means not spending our energy trying to control situations and events to suit ourselves, not being frustrated because things haven't gone the way we'd have liked. As Sister Jane of the Sisters of the Love of God, a person of a deeply contemplative spirit, wrote in a letter, 'We can always try to say "Yes" to whatever comes upon us in outer or inner life.'

It means that we can look for the hand of God even in the hard, unpleasant and frustrating things and say 'Yes' to God's working. It doesn't mean that everything that happens is good, or is all God's doing, or that we should simply be passive victims of what is done to us. Nor does it mean that we should be careless of the evils around us, or that we should do nothing to amend things that are wrong. Sister Jane adds: 'Of course, sometimes saying "Yes" means not being passive, as when one is called upon to try to change circumstances for oneself or other people.'

Often one of the most difficult things to accept is simply ourselves. If we feel that we are not what we would like to be, or what we think God wants us to be, this can leave us with a sense of guilt. And we may feel frustrated at our inability to change. Yet, paradoxically, it is when we accept ourselves as we are, with all our inadequacies and failures, and when we look away from ourselves and focus instead on God, that God is able to work within us to change us.

33.

Into Your Hands

WHEN we engage in silent prayer we put ourselves into God's hands. This is not just a letting go, a relinquishing of control or responsibility. It is a handing over, a positive and deliberate placing of ourselves in the hands of Another. In the stillness of prayer we hand ourselves over to God.

What does it mean to hand oneself over to God? It can mean to place ourselves under God's direction; to loosen our own tight grip on our lives, and our attempt to control events, and hand over control to God, looking for God to direct our ways. It can also mean to put oneself into God's safe-keeping and ask for God's protection. We do this in a special way at the end of the day, as we commit ourselves to God for the night. We may use the Psalmist's words, hallowed by our Lord's own use of them at the moment of death: 'Into your hand I commend my spirit, for you have redeemed me.'[48] Placed in the strong hands of God, we can find safety and protection, and can rest in peace.

But placing ourselves in God's hands is something more radical and total than just asking for protection and direction. It is handing over our selves, our whole existence and being, who and what we are, the 'I' that is at the centre of our lives, to God. It is acknowledging that we belong to God and that we no longer have possession of our selves, that our lives are not our own but God's. The poet of Psalm 31 acknowledges this when he commends to God the 'spirit' or breath within him that gives him life.

---

[48] Ps. 31: 5.

There is a paradox here. We give ourselves to God, but before we do so, we already belong to God. As the Psalmist commends himself into the hands of the God who has already 'redeemed' him, so we too know that we are already God's, as we hand our being over to God. We owe our existence to God. Our life comes from God, and it is to God that we will return. In Christ, God has claimed us for his own, and we belong to God. In our silent offering we hand back the self that is already God's, expressed in a hymn by George Matheson in these words: 'I give thee back the life I owe'.

We need to give back this life, and to go on giving it back—because we keep on resisting God's possession of us. We try to wrest control of our lives from God, and take them into our own hands. We behave as if our lives were our own to do what we like with. So we need constantly to come back to this silent offering, to handing ourselves back to God.

If silent prayer is genuine, it is always such an offering, a handing over of our total self to God. Through this self-oblation, we begin to discover that the God to whom we belong is our home and our deepest joy. We find that we do indeed come under God's protection. When our whole being is put into God's hands we are safe, because ultimately nothing can snatch us out of God's hand. And we also find that we do indeed come under God's direction and control, but that this control is not something rigid or arbitrary. God directs us, not by giving orders and expecting compliance, but by walking with us, in a relationship of warmth and understanding and love. When our lives are handed over to God, we find there is a freedom, a release from anxiety about ourselves. We walk with God in a free companionship, knowing that we belong to God.

THE PRAYER OF SILENCE

IV

WITH OTHERS ON THE HEART

34.

Torn and Broken Humanity

THE PRAYER OF SILENCE is not just a private matter between ourselves and God. While we are alone with God in our own inner solitude, we are at the same time united with the rest of humanity. Our silence links us with the world around us, and can become a deep form of intercession.

We need no reminder of the torn and broken state of the world. While clearly there is much that is good and admirable in human life, there is also much that is evil, in the form of suffering and in the form of wrongdoing. It is not hard to recognise that the origin of the wickedness of the world is the human heart, and what the old writers called our 'passions'. These are the often hidden and subtle ways in which human thoughts and actions are governed by selfish motives of greed, superiority, resentment, and love of power, leading to violence, injustice and uncontrolled hedonism.

In the course of silent prayer, as we enter our inner depths and hold ourselves still before God, we can be brought face to face with our own passions. We are reminded of the extent to which we inwardly seek to promote ourselves or to protect ourselves. As we look honestly at our inner selves, we learn that we are ourselves swayed by the same motives and urges, both good and bad, that move others and produce both selfless generosity and hideous cruelty in human life. Along with much that is good within us, the inner forces that trouble the world and play havoc with human life are also present in some measure, at least in potential. In other words, we ourselves are part of torn and broken humanity.

Silent prayer is the inner offering of ourselves to God. In the silence, we open up all that is in us and hand it over to God to be transformed. We offer to God not only our private, personal life, but also a part of the life of the world. Sadly, none of us can hope to achieve very much by our practical efforts to make the world a better place. But, if we persevere in the practice of silent prayer with honesty, faithfulness and commitment, and the self-offering this involves, we are taking responsibility for our own small share in the troubled state of the world. When we do this, one little bit of torn and broken humanity is laid before God, for God to take and transform. There is nothing more important that we can do for the life of the world, and no more effective form of intercession, than this.

The Christian Gospel tells of how God 'bears the sins of the world', how God in Christ has taken upon himself, and absorbed into himself, the woes and the wrongs of torn and broken humanity. This is God's way, and the only fundamental means of dealing with evil. In the mystery of the 'wonderful exchange' between God and human persons, we are invited to share in a small way in the priestly task of absorbing evil. We can do this by learning not to return evil for evil in the daily business of living, and by persevering in offering the whole state of our life to God.

This can be an important and meaningful part of the purpose of silent prayer. For some it can become a significant part of the purpose of their lives.

35.

Trust and Security

WE ARE often advised to trust in God. This is not always easy, especially when terrible natural disasters happen that wreak havoc with people's lives, or when we encounter troubles in our own lives. It can be hard to believe that God is in charge, and that we can trust God to make everything all right.

The phrase 'trust in God' is found frequently in the Bible, and especially in the Psalms. The Hebrew word for 'to trust' means 'to find one's security'. Trusting in God is not a matter of believing that God will prevent terrible or unpleasant things from happening. Our experience of life teaches us that God does not do that. It refers to something deeper and more inward than that. To trust is to know that, whatever happens, we are ultimately safe in God; and that, no matter how important other things may be for us, it is only God who provides absolute safety and security.

We have a tendency to seek safety and inner security in other things—in material possessions, in our own abilities, in the good opinion of others, in the success of our projects— and we tend to become dependent on these things for our sense of well-being. When they are in place we feel safe, but none of these things can provide complete security. That is not to say that we should not enjoy and appreciate the things of the world. But the only ultimate reality is God, and the only ultimate security is in God. Everything else in life is ultimately insecure, because it is transitory.

In so far as we invest our basic security in the things of the world, we put ourselves at the mercy of the world. We then lay ourselves open to being pulled this way and that and fragmented, looking for inner safety where none is to be found. We find that, instead of contributing to the peace and wholeness of the world, we are contributing to its brokenness and have become predators on life rather than healers. For the sake of the world around us, as well as for our own sake, we need to find our ultimate security in God.

How do we do this? We cannot do it by our own effort alone. We cannot just decide by an act of will to 'trust in God' and find our absolute security in God. We find our ultimate security by going down into God; not by seeking security itself, but simply by seeking God. This is where the practice of silent prayer comes in. In the prayer of silence we aim to go deeper and deeper into God; to open ourselves to God in the heart of ourselves, and let God take us down into himself. Since God is the only ultimate security, it is our being in God that constitutes security. The deeper we go into God, the more secure we are. We depend more and more on God alone.

As we go down into God, we begin to recognise that God is not above human life and controlling it, but underneath it and sustaining it; that God is below us, supporting us and suffering with us. This can affect how we look on God in relation to natural disasters. It can also affect our own personal relationship with God. In the depths of silent prayer we can find ourselves surrounded by God, contained, enfolded and held by God. This is a profoundly personal sense, something that we can know in the core of ourselves. By our silent prayer we can begin to discover an inner security which frees us to be open to other people and to life. In a world of tragedy and suffering we can become, to a small extent at least, not predators but healers.

36.

With Others on the Heart

THE PRAYER OF SILENT WAITING before God provides a basis for other forms of prayer, not least the prayer of intercession.

Intercession is not simply a matter of mentioning people and places in our prayers. To intercede—'to come between'— is to stand before God for the sake of someone else. Intercession involves placing ourselves before God, in the depths of our heart, and then including other people and concerns besides our own. It means, as Archbishop Michael Ramsey said, being with God with others on our heart.[49] It is not something done lightly, simply by mentioning names, since it involves our heart, our very being.

As we stand before God we need to have a particular attitude towards those whom we include, indeed towards all people. We cannot stand before God with others on our hearts if we see ourselves as superior to them. The intercessory attitude is one of seeing others as above us. It is a matter of 'under-standing' others; standing not above but below them. This is, of course, easier to do in relation to some people than others. We tend to feel that certain people are not as good as we are, and this feeling is at odds with our attempts to have them on our hearts as we hold ourselves before God.

If we are going to intercede, in the sense of being with God with others on our heart, we need to listen to our Lord's injunction: 'Do not judge.' This is not a matter of suspending our critical faculties, but of not condemning or blaming others; of refusing to look for their faults; of trying of overcome our natural tendency to feel pleased when people

---

[49] Cf. *The Christian Priest Today*, Michael Ramsey, p. 14.

whom we dislike go wrong. To have others on our heart as we stand in silence before God is to look away from their faults, just as we trust that God will look away from ours. It was said of the great Macarius, one of the most influential of the Desert Fathers, that 'just as God protects the world, so Abba Macarius would cover the faults which he saw, as though he did not see them; and those which he heard, as though he did not hear them'.[50] As we intercede we place our hands over the failings of others so that we do not see them. Only in so doing can we stand before God with others on our heart.

It is worth remembering that Jesus' only recorded instruction about praying for others is: 'Love your enemies; pray for those who persecute you.'[51] The depth of our intercession can be judged by whether before God we have on our heart those whom we dislike, those who have maltreated or offended us, and those who are the enemies of society and do evil things in the world. Another of the Desert Fathers, Abba Zeno, said:

> If a man wants God to hear his prayer quickly, then before he prays for anything else, even his own soul, when he stands and stretches out his hands toward God, he must pray with all his heart for his enemies.[52]

We recall that Jesus himself, before he commended his own spirit into the Father's hands, prayed for his persecutors.

Viewed in this way, the work of intercession is a deep and costly one, arising from our standing still before God in the depths of our heart.

---

[50] *The Sayings of the Desert Fathers*, trans. Sister Benedicta Ward SLG, Macarius 32, p. 134.
[51] Matt. 6: 44.
[52] *The Sayings of the Desert Fathers, op. cit.*, Zeno 7.

37.

Powerlessness

PEOPLE SOMETIMES speak of prayer being 'powerful'. But this is to misunderstand its true nature, for the most real and effective prayer is, in a sense, powerless.

This is because God works not by power, in our understanding of that word, but by powerlessness. Certainly God has power, and by it God created the heaven and the earth. Both the Bible and our liturgies ascribe power to God: he is the 'God of power and might'. But what we know of God, both from the Bible and from our own experience, is that he does not work in his world by the exercise of power. God's 'power' refers to the nature of his being, his unlimited ability and resources, not to his way of operating. It is not, as with human beings, the power of domination that forces people to do the will of God, but the hidden, mysterious power that works through weakness, as is seen in the Cross of Christ. As one biblical scholar has said, 'Weakness is the presupposition of the working of divine power.'

The Church of Christ is called to follow the way of Christ and to work through powerlessness. But, sadly, throughout its history it has been tempted by power. Too often, the Church has tried to gain influence and control over people and society, its leaders have sought power over other people, and its members have elbowed each other for power and control in congregations. There have, nevertheless, always been humble and powerless men and women of prayer, whose lives have probably constituted the most truly effective work of the Church.

The prayer of silence is a kind of powerless prayer. In it we lay ourselves before God, just as we are, and in doing so we place our weakness and emptiness alongside the powerlessness of God. We know that God uses our gifts and abilities, and it is right that we should offer these to God, but it may be that our weakness, and the acknowledgement of our powerlessness, is of more significance in God's 'strange work'. For this reason, we must be willing to own, and enter into, our own weakness and powerlessness.

There are different kinds of weakness. There is the weakness which comes to us through illness, disability, depression or old age. There is also the weakness which is an inescapable part of our nature. As we discover our inner selves, we realise our ultimate powerlessness and vulnerability. Underneath the knowledge, skill and power we need for living in the world, there is an inability to help ourselves. We cannot be all we would like to be, solve all our problems or extend the span of our years. We cannot control the behaviour of other people. Because of this powerlessness, both external and internal, we are all in one way or another vulnerable and open to hurt. Engaging in the prayer of silence involves going down deep into ourselves, acknowledging this powerlessness and vulnerability, and offering it to God. We offer it, not so that it can be removed or cured, but so that it can be taken up into the weakness and vulnerability of God as demonstrated in Christ, and so used for his purpose.

In the prayer of silence, we recognise that our prayer is not powerful in the world. As we hold ourselves before God for the sake of the world and other people, we do not wield power to influence events or change what is happening. Silent intercessory prayer is effective when, standing before God, we become in a small way channels for the mysterious work of the God who works by powerlessness.

38.

Offering the World's Life

EACH OF US is part of the wider world around us. When we come before God in prayer, we do not come alone, but as one component part of this many-sided world. If we offer ourselves to God in prayer, we are in a sense offering a part of the life of the world to God.

There is beauty and glory and loveliness in the world. And there is human love and kindness and fortitude. Having our share in all this means we can offer it to God. Seeing the wonder of the natural world around us, we can join in and offer its praise. According to the Psalms, the entire natural world celebrates and rejoices in the presence of God. The sea roars, the fields exult, the trees and the hills sing for joy, and the floods clap their hands. The mountains and hills, the fruit trees and cedars, the snow and frost, the animals and birds are all called upon to praise the Lord. In the light of this, we too can think of the whole universe standing and moving in reverence for God, from the blades of grass and the tiniest forms of life to the distant galaxies and the unimaginable miles of space. Perhaps in our silent prayer we can let ourselves be channels of the response of the created world to its Creator.

As part of this created world, human beings have their own inherent goodness and greatness. This, too, secretly resounds in praise of God. We have our own God-given glory that reflects the glory of God and, perhaps, in our silent prayer, we can let something of the unspoken praise of humanity pass through us. It is surely right that we, as the human crown of God's creation, should glorify the Creator in this way.

But if there is beauty and goodness in the world around us, there is also brokenness, hurt and shame. We do not need to be told that there is a vast amount of human suffering; nor that there is cruelty and greed and wickedness. The life of the world is burdened by its woes and tarnished and torn by its wrongs, and we are a part of this too. Perhaps, in our silent prayer, we can let some part of the cry of the world against its sufferings and its wrongs pass through us also. Maybe our times of silence can be times when we feel a little of the world's suffering, and acknowledge our own fragility and vulnerability in the face of it. Perhaps we may also find ourselves standing with shame and penitence before God because we know we have a part in the wrongs and evils of the world. All of this, our human vulnerability and our shared penitence, can be held before God in silence, and offered up for God to transform.

Can we, perhaps, see this as part of the work of Christ, who stood before God representing all of us and offering the praise and the sinfulness of the world to God, and who since then has drawn in so many others to share in his offering of the life of the world to God? This could give an extraordinary depth to our work of silent prayer.

39.

Deepening Prayer

THE IMPORTANT thing about prayer is not the amount of time spent at it, or even its content, but its depth. In the prayer of silence we seek to deepen our prayer. How do we do that? No doubt there are many ways, but here are some suggestions.

Perhaps the most important way to deepen our prayer is to try to focus more and more on God. It is easy in prayer to focus our attention on our own thoughts and concerns. It is, of course, right and proper that we should bring these concerns to God; and sometimes we need to do this before we can be still and concentrate on God alone. But at some point our prayer should turn simply to God and the holiness of God. If we make a practice of holding ourselves in silence for a little while in reverence before the mystery of God, remembering God's holiness, we shall probably find our prayer moving to greater depth.

Another way is to pray with sincerity and genuine feeling. Deep prayer is heartfelt prayer. It is easy to 'say prayers' without there being much real or deep feeling attached to them, but it is often much harder to reach down into our hearts when we pray. When prayer doesn't 'come', we find ourselves unable to do much more than 'go through the motions', but there are times when we can try to dig deeper, and open up that part of us which feels.

We can do this in relation to different aspects or subject areas of prayer. Our prayers of thanks can move from thinking of things for which we ought to be thankful to feelings of deep and genuine thankfulness. In a sense the particular things for which we thank God are only reminders of God's goodness and of our dependence on him. These reminders can bring us to the point where we hold ourselves still in quiet gratitude to God, so that our offering of thanks becomes a part of our silent offering of ourselves.

The same can be said of intercession. Perhaps more than any other aspect of prayer, intercession can become something routine, a matter of mentioning certain people or concerns because we have decided to pray for them, without there being much depth to it. To deepen our intercessions we may need to let ourselves feel for the people and situations we are praying for. This may happen naturally and easily. Some of those for whom we pray are people for whom we have strong feelings of sympathy or anxious concern. But sometimes it requires an exercise of imagination before we reach a level of feeling in our intercessions. If we can do so, our feelings for others can then become the gateway to a place where we hold ourselves in silence and in self-offering before God for the sake of others, handing over our feelings to be used for this purpose. In this use of our feelings, our prayers can be deepened until they are merged into our silent waiting upon God.

But this prayer of silent waiting can itself be deepened. For this to happen, we need to allow time. Few of us can enter the depths of silent prayer in a few snatched minutes. We need to let ourselves gradually go deeper, and slowly and gently be drawn into the secret place of God. Allowing ourselves time to attain a sense of deep stillness, however briefly, is an important way of deepening our prayer.

40.

Placed before God

SILENT OR CONTEMPLATIVE PRAYER is not something we engage in for our own sake. Contemplation is not a technique for achieving inner peace or wholeness, or a method of growing in spirituality. It is a looking towards God, a way of focussing on God, placing ourselves before God, and seeking to align ourselves with God's activity. As we hold ourselves still in prayer, we place everything before God, all that is going on in and around us. This includes the troubles we face and all that we feel is wrong in our lives.

We may find ourselves troubled or distressed by external circumstances, or by persistent physical pain. If we lay these feelings before God in the silence of prayer, our distress may not be removed, but God may transform or transfigure it, enabling us to see that, in some mysterious way, God is within the situation. God may speak to us through our trouble, enabling us to see it in a totally different light.

Or we may feel that we have been wronged or mistreated by others. Laying this before God means that we do not have to endure it alone. It is also a refusal to return evil for evil, to pay back the wrong, to get our own back or settle scores. It means being willing to hold the hurt, to carry the pain, to lift it up to God in prayer, rather than to hand it back to another. To do this is to bear the wrong in the way that Christ himself did and taught us to do; and so to neutralise a little bit of the evil that infects human life.

When we place our inner self before God, we may also become conscious of things that are wrong within us. Most of us are aware that our inner life is not just as we would like it to be. There are ingrained ways of thinking, feeling and being which don't seem to change; imperfections we can't put right; failings which persist; inner wounds we can't heal. Placing all this before God does not mean that we find ourselves instantly changed, but it can reawaken in us the realisation that God accepts us just as we are, with all our failings. In this way, we can begin to learn to accept ourselves as we are, and to leave it to God to heal and purify us.

When we do this we can also become aware that the wrong within us is part of the evil and injustice of the world around us. The wrongs that afflict humankind arise, as Jesus said, 'from within'—from the inner state of human beings, including ourselves. We are all part of the human race, and the torn and disordered part of us is a part of torn and broken humanity. In opening up our own inner selves in prayer, we are uniting ourselves with the rest of humanity. In acknowledging the wrong that is within us, we are placing before God our own little bit of the evil that afflicts the world in so many ways.

Seen in this way, silent prayer is a positive engagement with evil and wrong, rather than a way of furthering our own spiritual development, or a passive, resigned acceptance of things as they are. God's way of dealing with evil, embodied in Christ, is to bear, absorb and neutralise it. When we place the wrongs within and without us through self-offering before God in silent prayer, we are sharing, in a very small way, in this secret work of God.

41.

Deliver us from Evil

IN the concluding petition of the Lord's Prayer, which is also perhaps its climax, we ask God for deliverance from evil. World events often bring home to us afresh the reality of evil, and so they remind us of the importance of this prayer. In a world threatened by evil in many forms, we need to pray for deliverance.

When we pray, 'Deliver us from evil', we may be calling for help, crying to God to rescue us and the people of the world from the dangers which threaten us. This is, of course, good and right. The Psalms and other parts of the Bible are full of cries to God to help and rescue us in our need. And, faced with the reality and the consequences of evil, we find ourselves also praying for others, offering to God our compassion for those affected by the ravages of violence and the miseries of injustice, asking for deliverance for them. But the reality of evil calls also for a deeper kind of praying. Perhaps standing silently before God in deep, penetrating, soul-searching prayer is the most profound and important way of responding to and engaging with evil.

Such prayer involves openness to God. In it we focus not on ourselves, and not even on the needs of the world, but on God, recognizing that what matters in the world is not what we do, but what God does. In silence we open ourselves to the mysterious activity of God, acknowledging our human limitations and weakness, and making space for God's workings in us and in the world. In this way we provide a small opportunity for the power of God to turn tragedy into new life, and to use disaster to point us to a better way of living.

Such prayer involves humility and penitence. It is in silence and solitude that we can discern more clearly the truth about our own hearts and the nature of evil. In our silent waiting before God, we recognize that we have a part in the evils of the world and that the passions which bring about terror, disaster and war have their roots in the human heart, including our own. In this prayer we remain still before God, acknowledging who we are and facing the truth of what lies within us. With humility and penitence we ask God to root out the evil in us and in the world.

Prayer of this kind is costly. It involves penetrating more deeply into ourselves and facing the God whom we encounter there. It requires self-examination and acknowledgement of the things about ourselves that we would rather not admit. This can be painful. It involves patience and perseverance, being ready to wait for God, sometimes in darkness and emptiness. It is not an easy kind of praying. It is not cosy or instantly comforting, though it can lead to a deep comfort and peace. In this way we take our responsibility for our share in the world's evil and bear our own little bit of its cost.

This prayer of silent standing before God may seem to lack purpose. It is, however, the most basic and profound way of engaging with evil at the place where evil has its roots. Throughout the centuries, people of deep spirituality have recognized that the world needs this kind of prayer. Men and women who, in their silent contemplation, have entered deeply into the world's pain, and remained with it in God's presence, have been the surest human bulwark against evil.

42.

Confession

THE PRAYER OF SILENCE can be a form of confession. We tend to think of confession as a way of acknowledging our sins or misdeeds, the things we have done which we ought not to have done. Of course we all do some such things, and it is right to confess them. But most of us do not often commit flagrant or obvious misdeeds. We do not cheat, rob or harm our neighbour, or do things that are manifestly wicked. It may be that we seldom find ourselves aware of a burden for which we need forgiveness and absolution.

Perhaps we need to regard sin in a different way—not so much in terms of specific misdeeds, but rather as an inner state. This is what the Greek Fathers referred to as a *katastasis*, a state of the soul. The state of our soul is characterised by a variety of attitudes, motives, inner intentions and prevailing feelings. These are in part good and lovely. Attitudes of kindness and caring, feelings of compassion, motives of self-sacrifice, and a real desire for the good of others are to be found in some measure in everybody. But there are also unlovely things which are often hidden, perhaps even from ourselves: unconscious selfish motives, the desire to manipulate and control other people, self-centred attitudes, and feelings of envy, resentment or anxiety.

Confession is not so much a matter of listing our misdeeds, but of opening ourselves and the state of our soul to God. Confession takes place when we place ourselves just as we are before him. In the prayer of silence we lay bare and expose our inner selves, with all that is within us, the good and the bad, the lovely things and the shameful things, the bits we like and the bits we don't like, the things other people can recognise in us and the things no one else knows about. We do not need to be conscious of all these things ourselves, but only to hold ourselves openly and quietly before God, knowing that all our desires are known to God, and that no secrets are hidden from God.

This can be summed up in the words 'acknowledge' and 'offer'. In the prayer of silence we first acknowledge and accept what we are. We discern as fully as we can what is within us, and lay it open before God. Then we deliberately offer to God the whole state of our soul, the good and the bad.

Acknowledging and offering through the prayer of silence is not an alternative to confession and repentance: it is confession and repentance. To bare our inner selves in the sight of God is demanding, and sometimes uncomfortable. It is not an easy option. But, when we do it, we find that God accepts us just as we are, and it is this acceptance that constitutes forgiveness.

In accepting us, God takes whatever we offer, transforms it and uses it, changing and reforming us in God's own time and way. That is not to say that we are immediately made different. Our attitudes and feelings are deeply ingrained in us, and while we can, of course, bring about some inner changes, we do not have it in our own power to become different people. Experience teaches us that, even when we open ourselves to God, the state of our soul is not purified all at once. But by acknowledging and offering our inner selves, we make ourselves available for God's purifying work. As we persevere with the prayer of silence, our confession becomes the means of God's operation within us.